Travelling

the

Sacred Sound Current

KEYS FOR CONSCIOUS EVOLUTION

Deborah Van Dyke

TRAVELLING THE SACRED SOUND CURRENT

Published by

Sound Current Music

RR1, Box 251

Bowen Island, B.C.

V0N 1G0 Canada

604-222-0060

Edited by Maggie Pym

Book design, layout, typography by

EyeLevel Productions - Candace Sorrentino

Printed in Canada by Friesens Corporation

Canadian Cataloguing in Publication Data
Van Dyke, Deborah, 1955-
Travelling the sacred sound current
Includes bibliographical references.
ISBN 0-9687667-0-6
1. Sound--Therapeutic use. 2. Voice--Therapeutic use.
1. Title
RZ999.V36 2001   615.8'51   COO-911348-7

ACKNOWLEDGEMENTS

My deep gratitude to the host of angels who assisted in the manifestation of this book, with special thanks to Maggie Pym, Candace Sorrentino, Daniel Statnekov, Dorothy Williams and Ron Van Dyke. To The Great Ones Whose Presence lights my path and sounds in my heart, my eternal love.

For my parents Donald and Marion, whose love provided the vessel for my Soul's note to sound forth...
For my sons Matthew and Joshua, who, as artists of the Higher Evolution, carry on the flame...
And for open ears everywhere...

May the Divine Plan unfold,

the Keynote of Unity be sounded,

and the Victory Song be sung.

Foreword

It is always a difficult undertaking to illuminate what is generally regarded by initiates as an arcane or hidden understanding. Although numerous ancient human cultures from around the globe have perfected their own "sciences of sound," much of the old wisdom has remained obscure or unavailable to Western seekers. Couched in metaphor or buried in archaic texts, the alchemy of sound and its use for healing and self-realization has been difficult to access, and even when discovered, to fully comprehend. In her book, *Travelling the Sacred Sound Current*, Deborah Van Dyke has accomplished an important work with her decipherment and explication of harmonic knowledge from a wide spectrum of world cultures.

The sacred use of voice and breath, Sanskrit mantras, Hebrew and American Indian chants, overtones and harmonics...all are interwoven intelligibly and discussed by Deborah as the multi-colored rays of a basic understanding that emanate from a single source. Deborah's heart and soul-felt connection to the use of sound in healing is also explored in great depth with chapters on her experiential application of crystal singing bowls and Peruvian whistling vessels as instruments for healing with sound.

Augmenting and illuminating her own explanation and insight are quotes from the author's comprehensive gleaning of core sources such as the Sufi Hazrat Inyat Khan and the prophet Isaiah who have written or discussed the role of sound in healing and realization. Finally, Deborah presents a variety of specific practices, so that the reader has an opportunity to experience for him/herself a particular practice or "ray" of understanding. Whether embarking for the first time or a studied student of the esoteric, *Travelling the Sacred Sound Current* will touch and nourish the soul's longing for knowledge and connection to the whole. As such, Deborah's book is a deep transmission of great beauty.

Daniel Statnekov
Author, Animated Earth

PREFACE

A NEW ERA OF HEALTH CARE IS EMERGING ... Recent scientific research is confirming the ancient wisdom philosophies which are gradually infiltrating modern therapies. Psychosomatic research is showing us that being human is an amalgam of experience and molecular processes, based on a physical genetic template, directed by consciousness of the soul, and powered by the spirit driven changes in energy levels throughout living matter. The process of evolution and growing through life is a complex information transfer system between frequency modulated molecules. It is a self-developing dynamical system of flowing changes in energy states between molecules. We now know that even the genetic template can be modified according to environmental influences and thought processes. A healthy human expresses a free flow of balanced information transfer through resonating molecules and electromagnetic energy fluctuations. An imbalance in information processing, either through conscious awareness or subconscious influences, can result in many adverse physiological effects including an imbalanced autonomic nervous system, inappropriate levels of hormones and neurotransmitters, abnormal immunity, and ultimately changes in genetic expression. These changes, unless corrected, may result in mental and physical illness.

The role of sound in frequency modulation of molecular resonance and its influence on electromagnetic field fluctuations is important in restoring the balanced information transfer that is necessary for the maintenance of health. Deborah Van Dyke has written a delightful book and produced a beautiful companion soundtrack of chants, mantra toning, and rhythm, which can be used in meditation exercises for re-balancing the physiological processes in your mind and body. The book is poetic in style and saturated with quotations from the foremost mystics and ancient wisdom traditions. It imbibes more than knowledge, by creating an experiential, transpersonal journey through the mystical visions of the cosmic consciousness, and provides portals to connect with the divine. When the chapters are read concurrent with meditating to the soundtrack, the reader is able to experience the effects of sound on her mental status and physical well-being. Stress can melt away, and pain can be diminished, as a shift in consciousness takes place. Creative ideas, clarity of thought, relaxation and peace often emerge. Thousands of years of documented mystical experience have recorded the utility of expression, divine reverence, meditation, and sound in the maintenance of health and coping with illness. Now, scientific studies are confirming this truth. I highly recommend this book and the companion CD to health care professionals, their patients and, indeed, anyone who wishes to pursue a healthy lifestyle.

Stephen M Sagar, MD
Oncologist and Associate Professor of Medicine,
McMaster University, Hamilton
Founding Director of the Complementary Medicine Section of the Ontario Medical Association

TABLE OF CONTENTS

Chapter Six
PERUVIAN WHISTLING VESSELS

Chapter Seven
THE SOUND CURRENT

Chapter Eight
THE WAY OF CONSCIOUS EVOLUTION

Dear Reader,

     Travelling the Sacred Sound Current: Keys for Conscious Evolution is a sound journey encompassing multiple levels. It is a gathering of key teachings from Masters of Sound throughout the ages. It provides practical information and techniques for your personal application, as well as guidance on the esoteric uses of sound as a tool for healing and sacred creation.

     When one begins to work with the Sacred Science of Sound, a powerful force is invoked. As we elevate our vibration through sound, the spiritual fire in our body rises. This fiery stimulation loosens and dislodges energies of a denser nature, causing them to surface. Maintaining one's balance during this process is key and requires ongoing inner purification as well as physical exercise to aid in physical release and grounding. When practicing the sound exercises in this book, allow yourself time to integrate the new frequencies and gently release the old. Follow your inner guidance. Never continue past your own comfort level or that of others if working in a group. As you embark on this voyage, prepare for change, for sound is an efficient energy shifter that can facilitate deep and lasting transformation and provide entrance into the realms of Soul.

     The nature of sound is nonlinear; a vibratory wave that penetrates deep into the transcendental field of the listener, far deeper than written words are able, and thus the musical accompaniment: "*Travelling the Sacred Sound Current: Divine Chants & Sacred Tones for Healing & Meditation*" was created. This CD is a collection of Sacred Intentional Sound, inviting the listener to experience the Sound Current of divine mantras, chants, crystal bowls, drums, didjeridoo, chimes, gongs, nature tones and meditation.

     May you be blessed by the outpouring of higher harmonies that flow through the Sound Current and may you be inspired to sound *your* Soul's note in all its glory in your life. As you do, you transform not only yourself, but those around you. When enough of us are singing from our hearts with the voice of our Soul, a new song will unfold in a world thirsting for harmony.

     In the Silence between the Sound, may we find our return to the original peace of our Soul.

     Deborah Van Dyke

"The greatest science in the future, as it was in the beginning, will be the science of sound, harmonics, and music…this science will be given to those who will work to restore the Plan on Earth, or who are in harmony with the 'purpose which the Masters know and serve'."

From *The Creative Sound*
Torkom Saraydarian

"Sound is your essence."

Upanishads

"Wherever you are,
There!
Is the entry point."

Kabir

INTRODUCTION

I vividly remember lying in bed at night as a child before falling off to sleep, mesmerized by the sound of the wind as it blew through the trees. I was beckoned by the wind's many voices: during a storm its irrepressible, howling strength; on a warm summer's eve its gentle, soft whispers. Instinctively I would merge my consciousness with this ever-changing force and fly upon its currents of freedom, transported beyond the boundaries of my small human self to a place before words, a place of deep, soothing comfort. The wind's audible breath acted as a trigger, a "sound code" that stirred my awakening consciousness. This pure voice of nature spoke truth to me in the way of the Original Language: the language of pure vibration that is common to all things: every creature, every pine needle, every star.

Many years later I experienced a similar summoning when I first heard the resounding tones of a crystal singing bowl. As the sound vibrations of the bowl permeated my body, every cell began to tingle and sing in response. These pure crystalline sounds travelled deep within, touching long forgotten parts of my Self with their golden chords. Their sound vibrations opened doorways within my consciousness, setting me on a wondrous journey through the inner realms; a discovery of the "libraries within libraries" which are entered not through reading, but through direct experience.

Sound evokes such remembering. It speaks to our Soul in a way that nothing else does. It is intimate, it is visceral, it elicits feeling. The secret to its power is its ability to bypass our intellect and touch our emotions. Penetrating deeply through our innermost being, sound unifies our isolated pieces, restoring the harmony of the whole. Sound links us with a remembrance of our Soul's essence. An ancient Ren (Egyptian) teaching describes it thus, "Lifetime after lifetime our Soul Identity is awakened through sound…once heard, the Sound calls our Soul into the proper dimension and we begin to vibrate at the rate of our Soul Frequency."

Sacred sound creates a communication channel between the higher and lower kingdoms. It is a carrier wave that can transport us beyond the gateways of our known world to the timelessness of our inner essence and the symphony of the Cosmos.

"Beloved Behold Beyond Belief" are words I received in meditation on the path of sound…
Beloved…know you are truly loved, at the core you are pure love essence, the Original Tone that is Eternal.
Behold…the Great Harmony that unites all in Oneness.
Beyond Belief…the true essence of your Soul originates from the primal sound - far beyond the narrow confines of human belief, wherein lies your potential for unlimited creation.

The Tibetan Master, Djwhal Khul, whose teachings are revealed in the books of Alice Bailey, draws our attention to the profound role the science of sound will play in the unfolding of humanity's evolution, advising that it is *upon Wings of Sound* that *the Way of the Higher Evolution* is travelled.

Sound plays an inherent role in the transformation of our consciousness because it is the very vibrational nature of our Soul. Pythagoras and Plato taught that the nature of the Soul is music. Upon its wings we travel on our return path home. As we respond to this call home, we begin the process of purification and initiation through the spiritual planes of Sound and Light.

The intent of this book is to offer sound tools for the reharmonization of ourselves and our earth. These sound codes are a link to higher octaves of consciousness; the travelling wings for our Soul. When we travel the Sound Current, we are not travelling anywhere outside of ourself - we are travelling within. Our body is the gateway to All That Is.

"Sound lies within the heart of God. Sound is the most powerful force in all creation, carrying with It the power to transform.

Sound replaces our illusions with truth. It is pure consciousness Itself, the source of all lasting, creative endeavours,

and the deliverer of soul. It is indeed the force which liberates the beautiful butterfly of the soul from its cocoon,

freeing soul to live and unfold in a way heretofore unexperienced and only vaguely conceived."

From *From Light to Sound*
Dennis Holtje

The effects of sound span through the physical to the transcendental. On a physical level some of the measurable results displayed by the body in response to healing sounds are a reduction in blood pressure, respiration, and heart rate and the inducement of deep states of relaxation. Certain sounds such as the alpha waves produced by crystal bowls, can assist us in attaining dominion over our mind by stilling internal chatter and focusing our awareness. As a transformer of mind and emotion, sound becomes a vehicle for transcendent experience, a bridge between the formless regions of spirit and the physical world. It offers the keys to freedom referred to by ancient mystics and saints when they spoke of riding the inner "Shabd" or Sound Current, as the path returning them to Source.

"Far beyond Nad-Bad (outer music) lies the Anahat or the unstruck, self-supporting Music."

From *Naam Or Word*
Kirpal Singh

While listening to the "outer music" of nature, whether the natural harmonics produced by the wind blowing through the trees, the eternally joyful morning song of birds, the crickets' evening serenade, the soft rhythm of falling raindrops or the continual pulse of ocean waves upon the shore, we are reminded of our true origin. The pure sounds of nature originate in the higher realms and are mirrored here on earth. Our Soul recognizes these sounds from its home. We are drawn to the purity of their vibration because they remind us from where we came. All of our experiences with "outer music" are however, but preparation for us to be able to hear the "unending music" - the stillpoint of silence within the sound - with the inner ears of our Soul. As Kirpal Singh explains, *"The inner Music of the Soul is the real song. Its tunes are self-existing and self-supporting and need no outer aids of hands, feet or tongue and lead to the source from whence they come, the Minstrel divine."* This is the Sound Current which carries us Home.

> *"The whole world is reverberating with Sound,*
> *To listen to It thou must unseal thine inner ears,*
> *Then shalt thou hear an Unending Music."*
>
> …Shah Niaz

During meditation I received a vision of angelic sound chambers of high vibrational frequency and beauty on the inner spiritual planes. Functioning as transmitting stations, these chambers appeared to me as luminescent crystalline spheres emanating spiraling streams of pure vibration, tone and colour. I later read a passage from *The Book of Knowledge: The Keys of Enoch* by J. J. Hurtak, which describes the angelic emissaries serving on the higher realms as the Order of the Elim: *"The Order of the Elim represents the sustainers of the vibrations of sonic energy used in the music of the spheres…Through the use of diminishing chord structures, the Elim reactivate sound patterns of creation from one sphere to another…The Elim use spherical musical forms to inspire art, teachings and transformational activities in the realms of creation."*

Harmonic sound codes pulse continually through all dimensions of consciousness: sound codes that are designed to activate the inner hearing and memory of our Soul. As our inner ear awakens to hear beyond the mundane of the ordinary world, we begin to hear on the level of our Soul. It is with this Soul hearing that I invite you now to journey…

TONES OF CREATION

"The Universe was manifested out of the Divine Sound;

From it came into being the Light."

Shamas-i-Tabriz

VIBRATIONAL KEYS

"A tone lies at the foundation of everything
in the physical world."

From *The Inner Nature of Music and the Experience of Tone*
Rudolph Steiner

Sound and Light are the vibratory tones of creation. The Universe was built on tone. Take away the "t" and you have the keyword "one". The Universe was built on one.

"The Great Singer built the worlds, and the Universe is His Song" is an ancient Hindu expression. This concept is echoed in *The Hathor Material* by Tom Kenyon and Virginia Essene, *"...love is the highest vibration, the fundamental octave, the fundamental tone that resonates through the entire Universe and through all dimensions. This tone is the fabric that holds the worlds and atoms together."*

As vibrational beings we are a part of the harmonic song of the Universe, the result of intoning chords woven by our Soul to take its human form. Working with the love-tone worlds of Sound and Light, we can retune and realign the divine instruments of our bodies into atonement (at-one-ment) with our Soul and the original tone of Source.

In *The Music of Life*, the great Sufi Sound Master Hazrat Inayat Khan discusses the nature of Sound and Light, *"The nature of creation is the doubling of one. It is this doubling aspect that is the cause of all duality in life: one is positive, the other negative; one expressive, the other responsive. The first aspect is sound, and the next is light. In nature, which is face-to-face with spirit, what is first expressed is light, or what one first responds to is light; and what one responds to next, what touches one deeper, is sound."*

Sound is a conduit which enables us to travel beyond the mind-locks of our consciousness to the deeper regions of our Soul where the true Self is revealed.

All the world's great spiritual traditions recognize and incorporate the use of Sacred Sound as a means of guiding one back to the Divine:

CHRISTIANITY *"In the beginning was the WORD..."(St. John)* is the creation story in Genesis linking all of creation back to the original sound of the Logos...the Divine Word.

SUFISM *"The whole manifestation being the phenomenon of sound,*
the knowledge of sound is the key to the mystery." (Hazrat Inayat Khan)

TAOISM *"When the mystic virtue becomes clear, far-reaching,*
And things revert back to their source,
Then and then only emerges the Grand Harmony." (Lao Tze)

HINDUISM *"Muttering the sacred syllable 'Aum' rise above the three regions, And turn thy attention to the*
All-Absorbing Sun within. Accepting its influence be thou absorbed in the sun,
And it shall in its own likeness make thee All-Luminous." (The Gayatri from the Rig Veda)

JUDAISM *"Yod He Vav He"* is the sacred name mantra for the Divine Creator.

BUDDHISM *"The voice of the Sanskrit is the voice of the Cosmos. When the sounds of the Cosmos dissolve in your bloodstream,*
and cause your own body's sounds to harmonize with the rhythm and tempo of the notes of the Cosmos,
there will be a sublimination, a metaphysical transformation of your heart and soul, a unification with the Supreme."
(The Inner World of the Lake - Grandmaster Sheng-Yen Lu)

Sound is vibratory and sounds of high vibrational nature such as those used in spiritual worship, create a field of frequency, a channel for accessing the pure, rarefied energies of the Divine. We come from One Voice. We long to be reunited with this truth. When toning or chanting solo, I am connected through my sound with a great sense of oneness. This feeling of unity expands even further when I join with a group to create healing sound. The "union" of sound, created whenever two or more are gathered together, is a union of individual parts blending together into the harmony of One through their sound. Sound is a tremendous unifying force and when it is created with the intention of love and union with Source, it is one of the most powerful healing tools on our planet.

As foretold in *Esoteric Healing* by Alice Bailey, *"Healing by means of sound will be one of the first healing unfoldments to be noted at the close of the next century."* Edgar Cayce also predicted that healing with pure tone would become the most important healing tool of the 21st century.

Our world is composed of a myriad of sounds, some harmonious, some dissonant; those which initiate creation and those which bring about the dissolution of form. As Torkom Saraydarian, teacher of the Ageless Wisdom and Agni Yoga reminds us in *Cosmos in Man*, *"Let us not forget that sound is fire, and all that is related to sound is fiery. All your words, songs, chantings and prayers are fiery in nature, and when you are dealing with them, you must know that you are dealing with Fire. Fire is the agent of Cosmic Creativity, the agent of purification, and the agent of destruction."*

Groundbreaking research on the effects of sound on human cells, presented by Fabien Maman in *The Role of Music in the Twenty-first Century*, includes microscopic photography documenting the ability of acoustic sound to destroy cancer cells and vitalize healthy ones. The key to sound's vibrational power is found on the atomic level where its fiery energy penetrates and resonates in our cellular DNA. Recognizing that sound frequency is an inherent part of all substance in the Universe, we are beginning to comprehend the magnitude of sound's potential for healing on all levels. As yet we have only touched the tip of the iceburg...

"Since all things are made by the power of sound,
of vibration, so every thing is made by a portion thereof,
and man can create his world by the same power.
Among all aspects of knowledge the knowledge of sound is supreme,
for all aspects of knowledge depend upon the knowing of form,
except that of sound, which is beyond all form.
By the knowledge of sound man obtains the knowledge of creation,
and the mastery of that knowledge helps man to rise to the formless.
This knowledge acts as wings for a man;
it helps him to rise from earth to heaven,
and he can penetrate through the life seen and unseen."

From *The Mysticism of Sound*
Hazrat Inayat Khan

THE CREATIVE, ORGANIZING FORCE OF SOUND

"The creative process was initiated by Sound,

and in that Sound the Logos both invoked and evoked."

From *The Rays and the Initiations*
Alice A. Bailey

The biology of the unfolding universe has been described as having been initiated by a deep reverberation whose echoing sound waves brought about the formation of subatomic structure and subsequently, the atoms of human DNA.

Out of the silent peace of the motionless eternal came forth the activity of consciousness. We live in this sea of consciousness. This sea is a current of vibration that penetrates all existence. All matter is vibrational in nature. Every atom is constantly in motion and every vibration has its own frequency - its own sound. Sound is physics. Sound creates and organizes.

Scientist Dr. Hans Jenny saw the universe as harmonically connected. He was a pioneer in the field of "Cymatics" - the study of the dynamics of vibration that permeates our body and the world we live in. His book *Cymatics* reveals wondrous photographs of the intricate patterns created when liquid, sand and other various materials are exposed to different sound frequencies and vibrations. The geometric designs produced include lattices, spirals, honeycomb and hexagonal forms, and indeed it seems that we are being given a look into the very creational blueprint of the Universe.

Another demonstration of the magic of sound's creative power is found in the making of structured water with a crystal singing bowl. This is easily done by filling a crystal bowl half full with water and playing its rim with a rubber mallet. At first the water's surface begins to ripple and form a herringbone pattern, then effervescent bubbles begin to form which, as the sound increases, rise up out of the bowl creating a beautiful, spiraling, symmetrical fountain of water.

Harmonic vibrations
observed with a stroboscope

This provides clear, visible evidence of sound's power to organize matter. In the same way that sound rearranges the frequency of the water molecules, so does it affect and alter the vibration of the molecules of our human bodies.

"Since the difference between one dimension
of reality and another is its rate of vibration,
the key to the transformation of spirit
also lies within music."

From *From the Temple Within*
Evan T. Pritchard

We are on a path of conscious evolution when we begin to understand that we are bodies of living consciousness not bodies of matter. We are vibrational beings and sound is a vibrational key for shifting our frequency and accessing different levels of consciousness. Much like changing a television channel and tuning to a different broadcast, we can use frequencies of sound to retune our vibratory state to a new channel of harmony. Working with sound as a creative, organizing force we can restore balance, heal, and recreate ourselves.

"Substance develops from a ray to an atom,
but before this it exists as vibration."

From *The Music of Life*
Hazrat Inayat Khan

"The chief agency by which Nature's wheel is moved in a phenomenal direction is sound,
for the original sound or word sets in vibration the matter of which all forms are made and
initiates that activity which characterizes even the atom of substance."

From *A Treatise on White Magic*
Alice A. Bailey

"Vibration is the key to unlocking the Universe. Music can pull it apart or bring it together,
the sound of a song at the right second can stir Soul to silence or stir it into God-driven ecstasy.
There is music in the wind and in the sound of our own breathing.
Turn a word aside and you have poetry, modulate your speech and you have music,
sing notes and you have a tune, but sing your heart and you transform the world.
Music is a medium for consciousness in all its forms, be it love, power, wisdom,
freedom or insight, and consciousness transforms everything."

From *From the Temple Within*
Evan T. Pritchard

"All things being derived from and formed of vibrations have sound hidden within them,
as fire is hidden in flint, and each atom in the Universe confesses by its tone,
'My sole origin is sound'."

From *The Music of Life*
Hazrat Inayat Khan

"It is said: adau bhagavan shabda rashih, 'God originally manifested as sound.'
This primordial sound is called spanda, or vibration.
It created the universe and still pervades everywhere, continually vibrating.
Even modern physicists agree that there is a vibration reverberating ceaselessly at the center of the universe.
This vibration is the source not only of the universe, but of our entire being, and it pulses within us."

From *I Am That*
Swami Muktananda

"Hear the sounds of the creation of life.
For in this song, you will understand a symphony
and the symphony is the creation of every note,
harmonious in tone, brought forth to resonate with every other note.
The new octave that is born into your awareness is super-consciousness."

From *Earth Birth Changes*
St. Germain

"Each Initiation into the Mysteries contained

the question - 'Is thy ear open?'"

From *Fiery World, Vol. 1*
Agni Yoga Society

LISTENING

"Hear, and your Soul shall live."

Isaiah 55:3

"The world is filled with the Divine Sound, Open the portals of your ears;
Listen to the Eternal Sound; It is beyond the reach of dissolution."

Niaz Shah

"Life is a house made of sound and people are made from that sound. Since people are made of sound,
listening is important. To become a true human one must be conscious of listening and hearing the voice of
the Great Mystery speaking through everything, through the sound of a tree, or the bird flying overhead, or
the wind in the room, or someone breathing, or someone talking, or a moment of silence. The activity of
sound is what made the people. It is, therefore, simply through listening and using that listening and
paying attention, that one finds the guidance of the Great Mystery along the path of life."

From *Being and Vibration*
Joseph Rael

"The Lord is an ocean of limitless, boundless and all pervading void.
Unless we have complete silence within ourselves, our soul cannot experience that Silence out of which arises
the Voice of Silence or Shabd Dhun, by contacting which our soul becomes merged in Silence."

From *Philosophy of the Masters*
Huzur Maharaj Sawan Singh

"Silence is the altar of God."

Paramahansa Yogananda

"When we go into the inner chamber and shut the door
to every sound that comes from the life without,
then will the voice of God speak to our Soul
and we will know the keynote of our life"

From *The Music of Life*
Hazrat Inayat Khan

SOUND'S ESSENTIAL NATURE

"When great nature sighs we hear the winds
which, noiseless in themselves
Awaken noises from other beings,
Blowing on them
From every opening
Loud voices sound. Have you not heard
This rush of tones?"

Chang Tzu

Sitting on a pebble beach, my back supported by the stump of an ancient tree washed aground long ago by the power of the sea, I relax and listen to the sound of the waves' rhythmic pulsing upon the shore. The sound current of the ocean speaks to me. Not to my thinking mind. I feel it sink in deeply, its sounds breaking on my inner shores. I feel its pattern, the fluidity of its movement, each wave reaching further inside. I gaze out to the open water. As the sounds of the sea penetrate my consciousness I access its memories. Water holds memory, it is magnetic. Functioning as a storer and carrier of information, it is a crystal ocean of memory; a great receptive container; the ears of the earth. I sit and listen to the waves from distant shores whose vibrations sound from across the galaxies and resonate within the cells of my body. There is an instant recognition…

Waves break in white foam upon the hard surface of the rocky outcrops. The rocks are a metaphor for our mind - so often impenetrable and fixed in its way. Immobile. While the ocean dances, flows, yields; pulsing with the life force of the Mother. The elements express her different faces, her many natures. Life is the glorious play of elements with one another. The interplay of the ocean's waves upon the shore creates the Mother's beautiful song. Sound requires matter to resound. Without land and ocean, the wind would have no where to blow its secrets. From air and earth, the crackling fire is given life. The play of opposites creates a beautiful dance. A harmony is created out of their joyful play. This perpetual dance of vibration pervades all life. Out of this synthesis of elements interacting, the Great Cosmic Symphony plays to our listening ears.

Our ears are magnificent sonic gateways upon which we travel the lifestream of sound vibration. The art of listening can be developed to provide us with information on many levels beyond the physical.

We can hear, in the ordinary sense of the word, on a mundane level with little conscious awareness. We hear traffic noise, it registers as a peripheral background sound but makes no particular impression on us. We hear it unconsciously. We are constantly being bombarded with artificial noises from our modern world, so many that we have learned to selectively tune them out, to shut off our hearing.

Another aspect of hearing involves more active participation on our part. We listen to a professor lecturing and pay attention to the information because we are motivated. In this case, hearing is associated with the function of learning and the assimilation of information. It takes place on the mental plane.

A more advanced state of hearing occurs when we listen not only with our ears, but with our whole being. As a woman describing her first experience with crystal bowls aptly put it, "The sound is amazing. It turns my whole body into an ear!"

Yet another level of transcendental hearing takes place when we close our ears to all outside sounds and listen to the inner sounds with our etheric ears. This practice engages the receptive, intuitive faculties of our Third Eye in conjunction with our ears, to tune in to the "Sound Current" referred to by ancient Yogic traditions as the "Inner Shabd" or inaudible Divine Sound. If one were to draw two imaginary lines: one from ear to ear and one from the Third Eye to the back of the head, the center point where the two lines intersect is the approximate location of the pineal gland. This center is the cave of our mystic hearing. This level of hearing requires intense concentration and the ability to focus one's attention with such single-pointedness upon the inner realms, that all perception of the outside world temporarily ceases. Here, deep in the sanctum of one's innermost Self, the door to the Divine Sound and Light may open and be experienced audibly with the inner ears and visually with the Third Eye. (See Chapter 7, The Sound Current)

"The ear is man's strongest organ for his emotional growth in the world and the means of receiving by repetition in sound from the astral world, and through tone and archetype in the Spiritual Worlds. It is the means through which his inner perception is trained spiritually in the first steps for the great Ritual. It is tone which in moving sound onto the ear changeth the rhythm in the physical body affecting the sentient body, moving the ethers and bringing about the changing of chemistry on which desire, aspiration, prayer, vision, oneness with God become part of man."

From *Islands of Light*
Ann Ree Colton

It is significant that in the developing human fetus, the ear is the first organ in the body to reach full maturity at around 145 days. While still in the womb our ability to hear is as fully developed as an adult's! It is obvious that the ability to hear sound is of prime importance to the newly incarnating Soul.

Newborn babies recognize and respond to sounds during their development in utero. Sound triggers memory; if its mother loved a particular piece of music, a baby will remember her emotional response and display a similar affinity upon hearing it in this world.

A first-hand example of this occurred during recording sessions of the Crystal Voices "Sounds of Light" CD. My musical partner Valerie, pregnant at the time, had a strong heart resonance with the crystal bowl tones we were playing. Months later, during her labour and delivery, she played our CD to provide a soothing, vibrational background and gave birth to an extremely calm and peaceful baby. Shortly thereafter, whenever exposed to this recording, her baby actively responded with laughter and smiles and was soon creating overtone-like sounds of his own.

The Soul's essence is sound and it is fascinating to observe the role that hearing plays in the early stages of human life; a time when we are still very closely connected to our spiritual roots. The Soul navigates its way through the spiritual planes and becomes oriented to the physical plane by following sound vibrations. Within the womb a baby is immersed in the sound world of its mother's heartbeat, breath and voice, all of which provide vital information to the Soul.

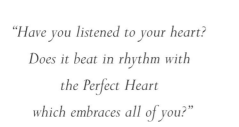

"Have you listened to your heart?
Does it beat in rhythm with
the Perfect Heart
which embraces all of you?"

From *Letters of Helena Roerich, Vol. 1*
Agni Yoga Society

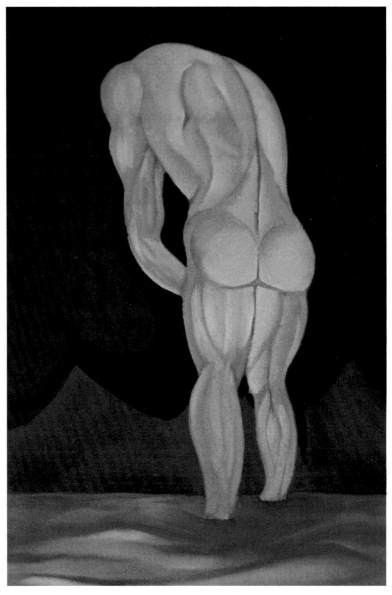

The Listening Pilgrim

"Listen, O Pilgrim, to the chanting of the Word by the great Deva Lords. Hush all earth vibration, still the restless strivings of lower mind, and with ear intent hark to the sounds that rise to the throne of the Logos. Only the pure in heart can hear, only the gentle can respond.

"The stormy sounds of all earth struggle, the shrill vibration of watery sphere, the crashing note marking the place of thought, dims the sound and shuts out the tone. He who is silent, quiet and calm within, who sees all by means of light divine … and is not led by light reflected within the threefold spheres, is he who will shortly hear. From out the environing ether will strike a note upon his ear unlike the tones that sound within the world terrestrial.

"Listen, O Pilgrim, for when that sound strikes in colourful vibration upon the inner sense, know that a point has been achieved marking a great transition.

"Watch then, O Pilgrim, for the coming of that hour. With purified endeavour mount nearer to that Sound. Know when its tone steals through the misty dawn, or in the mellow sunlight strikes soft upon the ear, that soon the inner hearing will become expanded feeling and will give place to sight and perfect comprehension.

"Know when the music of the spheres comes to you note by note, in misty dawn or sunny noon, at cool of eve, or sounding through the deep of night, that in their rhythmic tone lies secret revelation."

From *The Rays and the Initiations*
Alice A. Bailey

LISTENING EXERCISE:

In a world overflowing with sound, it is rare to experience pure silence. This exercise can be practiced while taking a bath; it allows us to mute out most external sounds and access the stillness of our private inner chamber. In a full bathtub, lie back with your head tilted in a floating position so that your ears are just submerged under the water. Close your eyes and relax in this warm, womb-like space. With most outside noise blocked by the water your attention is directed to the inner sounds of your body. Listen to your heartbeat and the sound of your blood running through your veins. All the wonders of the Universe can be discovered pulsing within our own blood. Hear the Voice of Creation in your body. Cultivate your awareness of the microcosm within. In the silence, listen…to the sounds of the inner planes of deep love, joy and remembrance. Begin to hear with every cell, opening to all the sound kingdoms within the body.

"In solitude the rose of the soul flourishes; in solitude the divine self can speak; in solitude the faculties and the graces of the higher self can take root and blossom in the personality. In solitude the sound is heard."

From *A Treatise on White Magic*
Alice A. Bailey

"Within the sound of your voice are the keys to innumerable worlds"

From *The Hathor Material*
Tom Kenyon & Virginia Essene

SELF-GENERATED SOUND

THE POWER OF VOICE

"Your voice links the conscious and unconscious levels of your being."

From *The Book of Sound Therapy*
Olivea Dewhurst-Maddock

The channeling of our voice energies to create sacred sound through song, mantra, chant, vowel tones or harmonic overtones, summons our attention into the present moment. It raises our vibratory rate and creates a bridge for accessing other dimensions of consciousness. When we consciously create sound with a spiritual intention, we are bathing our energy body in these higher frequencies and aligning ourselves with these fields. Thus our voice becomes our "ticket" for higher spiritual travel.

"The secret of return of Soul to Its origins is found in sound and song. The physical body too is vibration and responds to the music around and within it, especially if it is made to produce the sound itself. Although it remains physical, by singing a certain pitch and word, it can attune to any given vibration and open the door to that plane by sympathetic resonance."

From *From the Temple Within*
Evan T. Pritchard

People often have feelings of self-consciousness arise when toning or chanting in a group for the first time. Brought up in a culture that emphasizes the performance and entertainment aspect of music, most of us have had limited exposure to sound's higher vibrational value. Only now are we coming to understand the powerful healing medicine which sound offers. Every person has a unique voice - a signature tone that holds the imprint of their Soul's frequency like a fingerprint. Our Eternal Mother/Father knows us by the unique vibratory note we sound forth.

Sound that emanates from our pure heart and Soul creates a golden chord that links us to our path home. It is our God Channel. It matters not whether we are singing in perfect pitch. We can be tone deaf and yet initiating a sound which is sweet and pure and holy because it originates from our heart and it will be heard as the most joyous, beauteous tone because it flows from our sincere desire to be in communion with Source. This is the true power of our voice for when we make sound from this place, we emit sound which holds and carries this frequency and which, as it spirals outward, imprints every atom of consciousness with its tone and intention.

"The human voice carries the energy of the level where the
consciousness or awareness of the singer is anchored.
If he is in contact with his Soul, he will transmit the energy of goodness, beauty, and joy.
"If he is in contact with his Spark, he will transmit power - the energy of righteousness and principle.
"If he is in contact with the Hierarchy, he will sing about the Plan.
"If he is in contact with Shamballa, he will sing about the mysteries of
Shamballa and transmit the fire of Shamballa."

From *The Creative Fire*
Torkom Saraydarian

"*Once emitted, a sound goes on eternally and travels through the cosmos, influencing all the beings it encounters.*"

From *The Secret Music of the Soul*
Patrick Bernhardt

"…the worlds are the effect of sound"

From *Letters on Occult Meditation*
Alice A. Bailey

SOUND ~ THE CREATOR GOD

"In the beginning was the wind. With its whirl, it created the gjatams,

the primordial forms and the prime base of the world. This wind sounded;

thus it was the sound which formed matter. The pounding of these first gjatams brought forth further forms

which, by virtue of their sounds, in turn created new shapes. That is by no means a tale from days long

passed, it is still that way. The sound brings forth all forms and all beings.

The sound is that through which we live."

Old Lama in Tibet, as told to Alexandra David-Neel
From *Moenche und Strauchritter*

From the ancient Vedic tradition comes the term "Nada Brahma" which means "Sound – The Creator God". Common to creation stories of all cultures is the theme that the Creator manifested the world through sound. Indeed we are all creators and we are constantly projecting through our thoughts, the words we speak, and the tone of our voice, frequencies that may be either harmonious or chaotic, beneficial or destructive. Our voice is our most powerful instrument of creation and we must use it wisely if we are to become conscious co-creators in alignment with the highest good for all.

When asked to comment on how it was that the Hindu musician, Tansen was able to light candles by his singing of the Dipak Raga, Hazrat Inayat Khan replied, *"It is told that Tansen, the great singer, performed wonders by singing. Tansen was a Yogi. He was a singer, but the Yogi of singing. He had mastered sound, and therefore the sound of his voice became living, and by his making the voice live everything that he wanted happened. Very few in this world know to what extent phenomena can be produced by the power of the voice. If there is any real trace of miracle, of phenomena, of wonder, it is the voice."*

Our voice has tremendous generative powers; it is our natural, God-given tool for creation. When we tone with our voice, we are bringing forth the creative music of our Soul.

Soundwaves travel simultaneously in all directions from their source. When you generate sacred sound through your voice with a healing intention, you become a transmitting station broadcasting frequencies that travel around the world and throughout space. This is how our earth will be returned to harmony. We are only beginning to tap into the tremendous generating power of sound. As we learn to harness this power and use it with highest intention, we will alter and raise both our personal and world consciousness.

"What the initiate is learning to do is to make sounds consciously,
and thus produce a studied and desired result;
to utter words, and be fully aware of the consequence on all planes;
and to create forms and direct energy through sacred sounds,
and thus further the ends of evolution."

From *Initiation, Human and Solar*
Alice A. Bailey

TONING

"The purpose of all Toning is to restore the vibratory pattern of the body to its perfect electro-magnetic field, so that it will function in harmony within itself."

From *Toning - The Creative Power of the Voice*
Laurel Elizabeth Keyes

"Every living thing has its pattern of perfection upon which it was formed…It is natural to be healthy and happy. If there are malformations or disease, it is an indication that something has disturbed the pattern. Healing is a matter of removing the coating which hinders the natural flow of white light expanding out from the nucleus…

"The proper use of the voice is a means of directing the forces in our field to unite with their perfect pattern so that we may function in harmony."

From *Toning - The Creative Power of the Voice*
Laurel Elizabeth Keyes

"Toning, indeed, offers endless possibilities; in particular, its restorative value. It is the ability of giving release and allowing the natural flow of energy to move through one's body. It acts as a stimulator, removing the obstructions so that the body may function in its proper state. Toning is much more than just a release of tension. It acts as means by which the total expression of harmony and balance may be created and developed. It matters not whether an individual believes in it or not for toning deals directly with energy vortexes. These can be disturbed by the smallest vibration from feeling or sound, eventually to manifest as form. This, in turn, affects the electromagnetic energy of the individual. Thoughts by everyone are literally thrown into an energy force, creating either positive or negative frequencies. One can well understand that since we are living amidst a 'sea of personalities' it is important and essential to clean and re-establish our field pattern each day.

"There operates within the body vehicle a musical scale and when it is allowed to 'sing' forth in total freedom then are we attuned to the "music of the spheres"…that vibrational movement of our own creation. This form that we reside in was 'made manifest' in the light of harmony, not in the sufferings of discord. So arise each day in joyous enthusiasm and know always that each word we speak or sound we make (all thought patterns) sets in motion either harmony or discord in our lives."

Elyse Betz Coulson
From *Toning - The Creative Power of the Voice*
Laurel Elizabeth Keyes

"When you allow sound to move through you, it unlocks a doorway and allows information to flood into your body. It also penetrates the ground, affecting the vibrations of Earth and allowing a rearrangement of molecular alignment of information to take place...

"When you create harmonics of sound, it reminds your body of something. It reminds your body of light, of deep cosmic love, and of other worlds. Your body comes into joy and sometimes overwhelming sadness. It seeks and accesses a frequency that it has been longing for, which the sound has reminded it of. As you allow sound to play your body, you discover a frequency you have sought...

"Sound is going to evolve. Now human beings can become the instruments for sound through toning...These harmonics can be utilized in incredible ways...When you tone with others, you have access to the group mind that you did not have prior to making the sound. It is a gigantic leap in consciousness. The keyword is harmony. When the entire planet can create a harmonic of thought, the entire planet will change. That is what you are working for. You are going to broadcast a frequency, and that sound is going to travel. It is going to become a desperate aching and longing for a return to harmonics within the human race - a return to the power of the group mind and the simultaneous empowerment of the individual."

From *Bringers of the Dawn*
Barbara Marciniak

THE SACRED POWER OF VOWELS

"The euphonious sounding of the seven vowels is a way of reflecting the wholeness
of the creative vibration that has formed the cosmos, the planets."

From *The Mystery of the Seven Vowels*
Joscelyn Godwin

*T*oning offers a great key for the restoration and regeneration of the physical body. When we tone, we can bypass the mind and access the pure vibrational energies through which attunement is received. The toning of elongated vowel sounds ~ *UH, OU, OH, AH, II, EH, EE* ~ activates a deep Soul resonance in our body. Edgar Cayce spoke of the ancient Egyptians using the seven vowels to vitalize the body's energy centers.

Koto Tama is an ancient science of the "pure sound of the Soul" which has been transmitted by word of mouth down through the ages. It recognizes vowels as holding the magnetic, spiritual powers of the Soul that link us with the energies of space and the Cosmos, while consonants are understood to represent the electrical, physical energies that link us with time.

In many of the original languages such as Sanskrit, Hebrew and Native American Tiwa, the vibrational powers of vowels are considered a vital key for accessing universal energies. The tonoscope is an instrument invented by Dr. Hans Jenny that converts sound vibrations to visible patterns. Using this device, ancient Sanskrit and Hebrew vowel sounds produce the physical shape of their *written* symbols. When OM is toned into a tonoscope, an image identical to the design of the Sri Yantra is magically produced! The Sri Yantra (or Yantra of Creation) is the Buddhist mandala for OM.

The Kabbalistic chanting of particular vowel sounds is practiced to connect the chanter with divine energies. Through the chanting of what has been termed "the master code of A E I O U", one can access a fully "cosmated" consciousness. As William Gray, well known for his study of the Western Mystery Traditions describes in *The Ladder of Lights*,

"The vowels were 'extras' in Hebrew, and fitted in with consonants, formed words in order to give those words their real meaning according to the spirit in which they were intended. The vowels were originally very special sonics indeed, being mostly used for God-names and other sacred purposes. Consonants gave words their bodies but vowels alone put soul into them. Taken together in combination, the vowels will spell the Name of the Living One: I.A.O., I.E.O.A., HU, YAH, etc. Whichever way they are connected, they signify Divinity enlivening Existence, and hence were sacred in all Magical practices…"

Sufism also recognizes the powerful effect vowels have in awakening consciousness in the body. Each vowel is understood to embody the qualities of one the elements (earth, water, fire and air). In *The Music of Life*, Hazrat Inayat Khan relates the Sufi understanding of the qualities that certain vowels are said to hold: *E & I* are considered "jemal", the embodiment of a feminine, receptive, graceful essence, *O & U* are considered "jelal", the embodiment of a masculine, expressive, powerful essence, and *A* is considered "kemal" representing a balanced blend of feminine and masculine perfection.

In Taoist practice, the combination of toning certain vowel sounds and the visualization of certain colours is directed to the five major organs of the body to eliminate the crystalization of negative energies and maintain healthy functioning: *EH* and the colour *RED* toned into the heart, *EE* and *YELLOW* toned into the stomach, *OU* and *WHITE* toned into the lungs and large intestine, *OH* and *BLUE* toned into the kidneys and reproductive organs, *AH* and *GREEN* toned into the liver.

As practiced in ancient times of Atlantis and Egypt, vowel sounds can be used to tone a flow of revitalizing energy through our chakras. There are various systems that associate specific vowel tones with specific chakras, however, my experience has been that the entire body functions as a sounding board. By intoning each of the vowel sounds: *UH* (as in the), *OU* (as in blue), *OH* (as in toe), *AH* (as in father), *II* (as in eye), *EH* (as in say), and *EEE* (as in bee), the body vehicle and its chakras will naturally absorb what is needed, wherever it needs it. We simply need to follow our own intuitive guidance. Our body is a dynamic, constantly changing energy system that resonates to different sounds and pitches according to its current state. Sometimes we may be drawn to making very deep, guttural tones, at others it may be high pitched, angelic tones. Your body knows what sound it wants to make if you just allow yourself the freedom to play.

In his wonderful book *Being and Vibration*, Joseph Rael, known as Beautiful Painted Arrow, shares the essence of his native language Tiwa. He describes Tiwa as an original language of sound vibration, for which there is no written form, that has been passed down verbally through the generations: *"…a language that was constructed according to the different*

vibratory levels of mother nature." He speaks of the deeper energies behind each vowel sound: *"AAH - Purification, EH - Relationship, EEE - Awareness, OH - Innocence, the Infinite Void, UU - Carrying".*

Joesph suggests the following way of preparing ceremonial space through the toning of vowel sounds in the four directions: *"Face the East, and purify yourself with the sound 'aah'. Turn to the West and repeat the sound 'eee' to bond you with all things and all of the eternities and to connect you to the physicality of all things in that moment. Face now the direction of the South and sound 'eh' that you may be related to yourself and others. Turn to the North and sound 'oh' to connect to spirit, the breath of everything."* I use this simple yet powerful toning to create sacred space in a group; invoking the powers of the four directions with sound purifies, harmonizes and aligns the energy fields of individuals and the group as a whole. In the silence between the sounding of each direction, you can feel the energies coalesce within yourself and the group energy field.

BREATH ~ THE ESSENCE OF SOUND

Within the science of breathing lies the secret to all our creative work; that which can lead us "…*out of the phenomenal world into the kingdom of the Soul*." (*A Treatise on White Magic* by Alice A. Bailey) With our vitalizing breath, we breathe forth our intentions into the world. It is, therefore, paramount that we are mindful of what it is we are giving life to, what we are stimulating with our breath.

Toning originates from our living breath. The sound of our toning resembles the sound of wind blowing through a cave. Our mouth is likened to a cave and our breath is the wind upon which our created sound is carried forth. We exhale our life energy (the prana, chi, or mana) through our mouth and breathe or enliven our creation into being.

"*When one breathes out, it is the out-breath; when one breathes in, it is the in-breath. And the inter-breath is where the out-breath and the in-breath meet. The inter-breath is the same as speech. One speaks, therefore ,without breathing out or in.*" (*Upanishads*) The pause or stillpoint between the incoming and outgoing tide of our breath is the space from which our sound originates. Our breath is the very essence of our sound. Once again the *Upanishads* proclaims, "*Brahman is breath …Brahman is speech.*"

We can practice conscious breathing by holding an awareness that with each in-breath, we are returning to Source and being charged with Divine Love, and with each out-breath, we are outpouring this Love to the world. The real power of toning is allowing the breath of our sound which has been infused with our heart energy, to emerge.

When toning, it is important to breathe deeply into your abdominal center, allowing your stomach to fill with as much air as possible, much like a balloon expanding. This deep breathing propels your sound with energy sourced from the Dan Tian, a key energy center located by the lower abdomen. The Dan (Elixir) Tian (Field) is known in Taoist practice as the stirrer of Qi or life-force. When we tone with breath originating from this place of power we create sound which is charged with our vital life force.

*"Sound, light, vibration, and the form blend and merge, and thus
the work is one. It proceedeth under the law, and naught can hinder now the work from going forward.
The man breathes deeply. He concentrates his forces, and drives the thought-form from him.*

The Creative Work of Sound

The Science of the Breath"

From A Treatise on White Magic

Alice A. Bailey

"If there is anything that connects the mortal with the immortal, it is this bridge we call breath."

From The Music of Life

Hazrat Inayat Khan

"Mantra - A set of sound patterns and thought-forms which can code consciousness into the consciousness of Light. The mantras are holy energy forms of meditation which are used to charge the body with the powers and rapture of the Divine Mind."

From *The Book of Knowledge: The Keys of Enoch*
J. J. Hurtak

"MANTRAM - The speaking prayer in which the vowels and combining of words build the power to align one with the spiritual helps within the Spheres and Realms of Light. The sounding of word-combinings to dissolve karma, tension, and fear. A mantram contains molecular energy-particles of light. A mantram spoken with love and absolute belief is a freeing way."

From *Islands of Light*
Ann Ree Colton

HEALING MANTRAS

"Every mantra is multi-dimensional and can be applied to various planes of experience. Therein consists its living value and its creative faculty."

From *Creative Meditation and Multi-Dimensional Consciousness*
Lama Govinda

*T*he enunciated sounds of our spoken words bring our thoughts into form and are a powerful, magical, creative force. A mantra is the rhythmic arrangement of words or syllables that generate a specific vibration, creating a kind of etheric conduit between the chanter and the energies invoked. As Master Djwhal Khul explains in *Letters on Occult Meditation*, *"A mantra, when rightly sounded forth, creates a vacuum in matter, resembling a funnel. This funnel is formed betwixt the one who sounds it forth and the one who is reached by the sound. There is then formed a direct channel of communication."*

The word mantra originates from the Sanskrit words: manners (mind) and tar (to protect/free from). Mantras are imbued with specific vibrations inherent in them that can free our mind and connect our consciousness with the specific energies invoked. Mantras can be used as a purification bath; to cleanse our aura of dense, out of tune vibrations. There are many sacred mantras for tuning oneself to resonate with higher universal vibrations. Two of the most universally used sounds through the ages are OM - the quintessential cosmic sound vibration and HU - said to ground the highest celestial resonance on earth.

"The potency of a mantram depends upon the point of evolution of the man who employs it. Uttered by an ordinary man it serves to stimulate the good within his bodies, to protect him, and it will also prove of beneficient influence upon his environment. Uttered by an adept or initiate its possibilities are infinite and far-reaching."

From *A Treatise on Cosmic Fire*
Alice A. Bailey

Sound Exercise:

In *Creative Meditation and Multi-Dimensional Consciousness,* the much loved teacher of Tibetan mysticism, Lama Govinda explores the significance of the mantric seed syllables: OM - AH - HUM - HRIH, as they correspond to the movement of the elements. The toning of these four bija mantras is a powerful daily practice:

OM   "O" - the opening to the infinite. The primordial sound of timeless reality, purity and potentiality. A circular, all-embracing movement associated with the crown chakra and the element of ether.

AH   "A" - the first sound of creation. The expression of awareness, wonder, and inspiration. A horizontal movement associated with the elements of earth and air and with communication of the throat chakra.

HUM   "U" - universal wisdom reflected on the human plane, the eternal in form. The descending movement of ALL into the place of realization, the human heart chakra. Associated with the element of water.

HRIH   "I" - the highest spiritual vibration of all vowels, the greatest intensity of energy. The wisdom of the Third Eye chakra's inner vision. The upward, ascending movement of the fire element. The flame of devotion.

"The fifth chakra at the base of the throat is the chakra used by the Holy Ghost; this is where Shiva and Shakti marry or meet. The fifth chakra works in unison with the Bindu center at the base of the skull...Here, ether and akash unite as a virile and vibratory vehicle, that the music of God may be heard, and that all forms containing Bija or seed-sounds may conjoin and energize one another within the substances of life.

"The power of the Holy Ghost is the energy power of the Spirit of God, which can be heard by those having an ear as great musics or as a voice. The open inner ear is always accompanied by healing through speech. Through the use of the mantra and mantram, chanting and music, one unites with the akash Holy-Ghost Sound Current, and becomes a manifestor harmonizing the energy processes in the world, in the body, in the motions, in the mind.

"To open the fifth chakra, and to receive its illuminative benefits, is to become a powerful channel for God, a mediator and a manifestor. Vibrational God becomes Vibration within the akash center or fifth chakra. To speak a mantra, a mantram or a prayer; to sing of God; to praise God; and to resound the truth of faith - is to be a disburser of good tiding, of peace."

From *Kundalini West*
Ann Ree Colton

HU

The Sufi's consider HU (Hu-man) to be the most divine of all sounds. Hazrat Inayat Khan explains in *The Music of Life*:

"The Supreme Being has been called by various names in different languages, but the mystics have known him as Hu, the natural name, not manmade, the only name of the Nameless, which all nature constantly proclaims. The sound Hu is most sacred. The mystics called it the name of the Most High, for it is the origin and end of every sound as well as the background of each word. The word Hu is the spirit of all sounds and of all words, and is hidden within them all, as the spirit is in the body. It does not belong to any language, but no language can help belonging to it. This alone is the true name of God, a name that no people and no religion can claim as their own. This word is not only uttered by human beings, but is repeated by animals and birds. All things and beings proclaim this name of the Lord, for every activity of life expresses distinctly or indistinctly this very sound. This is the word mentioned in the Bible as existing before light came into being: 'In the beginning was the Word, and the Word was with God, and the Word was God'."

"Keep chanting the syllable HU while you are in the body. This word HU raises your vibratory rate, which is the secret to inner travel. Your vibratory rate determines what area or plane you will 'tune in' to at that time. Your vibratory rate also determines much of what and whom you experience during the day."

From *From The Temple Within*
Evan T. Pritchard

SOUND EXERCISE:

Close your eyes. With an intention of connecting with the sacred energies expressed by HU, take a deep breath into your belly and as you exhale, make a long, slow sound of "HHHHUUUUUUUUU". Repeat at least 10 times following the natural rhythm of your breathing. Be gentle as you tone, do not force the sound but allow yourself to be the vessel through which the frequencies of HU may emerge through your heart and throat. After toning be in silence, allowing the energies to be integrated into your body. This period of silence is essential for the assimilation of the sound.

AUM & OM:

FUNDAMENTAL VIBRATIONS
OF THE COSMOS

"Aum is the Creative Word, the whir of the Vibratory Motor…"

From *Autobiography of a Yogi*
Paramahansa Yogananda

"In meditation on AUM,
(A - Breathing in equals I COME FROM GOD)
(U - Holding the breath equals I EXIST IN GOD)
(M - Breathing out equals I GO BACK TO GOD)."

From *The Sacred Word and Its Creative Overtones*
Robert C. Lewis

"The energy of OM is like an infinite ocean
Moving in all directions
It pervades all, both inside and outside.
In the form of the higher mind,
It becomes creation, preservation,
And dissolution -
It becomes soundless.
The unstruck sound merges in the higher mind.
The higher mind dissolves in the OM sound"

From *The Sky of the Heart*
Nityananda

"OM sounded forth, with intent thought behind it, acts as a disturber,
a loosener of the coarse matter of the body of thought, of emotion, and of the physical body.
When sounded forth with intense spiritual aspiration behind it, it acts as an attractive medium,
and gathers in particles of pure matter to fill the places of those earlier thrown out."

From *A Treatise of White Magic*
Alice A. Bailey

"...if your ear is clogged with the noise of negative emotions, conflicting thoughtforms, habits, selfishness, pride and many kinds of vanities, you cannot expect to hear the Voice of Silence, the OM. The OM is the magnetic pull of your Angel calling you back to your Source through detachment, release and freedom.

"When your ear is cleared of the noises, you are ready to hear your Soul note, the note of liberating energy. The question may be asked, 'Should we sound the OM before we reach such a state?' The answer is, 'Yes,' because it is through striving toward the core of your being, and through the effort to reach your Source by cleaning poisons from the outside by sounding the OM, that eventually the inner OM and the outer OM meet and synchronize."

From *Cosmos in Man*
Torkom Saraydarian

"In sounding OM the walls of matter crack...The OM not only unifies and aligns you with your Higher Self, but it creates a symphony of colors which attracts the attraction of the devas of the spheres. These beings transfer more blessings and peace to you and cause expansion of consciousness. Also, as your note stablilizes and finds its own true key, your Master turns His eye upon you and you are gradually permitted to enter into His holy classes in the subjective levels."

From *The Science of Meditation*
Torkom Saraydarian

TUNE IN WITH THE COSMIC SOUND

"Listen to the cosmic sound of Aum, a great hum of countless atoms, in the sensitive right side of your head. This is the voice of God. Feel the sound spreading through the brain. Hear its continuous pounding roar.

"Now hear and feel it surging into the spine, bursting open the doors of the heart. Feel it resounding through every tissue, every feeling, every cord of your nerves. Every blood cell, every thought is dancing on the sea of roaring vibration.

"Observe the spreading volume of the cosmic sound. It sweeps through the body and into the earth and the surrounding atmosphere. You are moving with it, into the airless ether, and into millions of universes of matter.

"Meditate on the marching spread of the cosmic sound. It has passed through the physical universes to the subtle shining veins of rays that hold all matter in manifestation.

"The cosmic sound is commingling with millions of multicolored rays. The cosmic sound has entered the realm of cosmic rays. Listen to, behold, and feel the embrace of the cosmic sound and the eternal light. The cosmic sound now pierces through the heartfires of cosmic energy and they both melt within the ocean of cosmic consciousness and cosmic joy. The body melts into the universe. The universe melts into the soundless voice. The sound melts into the all-shining light. And the light enters the bosom on infinite joy."

From *Metaphysical Meditations*
Paramahansa Yogananda

"On the highest mountain can be heard, recorded and experienced the White Silence,
speaking to the ear hungry for the OM.
When the radiance of the soul is united to the One within the Om,
the White Silence becomes archetypal Joy, the Ecstasy.
Out of timelessness is the Word-vibrationless,
awaiting to speak to the receiving Archetone-points in consciousness.
In the White Silence, be all listening, all cognizant
The bell of the White Silence sounds, tolls, speaks to the need to know, to heal, to teach. OM."

From *Kundalini West*
Ann Ree Colton

In *Tantric Quest*, Daniel Odier relates his experience chanting AUM deep in the Himalayas with a great female yogi and teacher of Shivaic Tantrism, Devi:

"We spent two or three hours a day repeating the mantra AUM in one voice, slow and deep, feeling each low frequency vibration throughout the rest of the body, like the sound box of a stringed instrument. At first, Devi accompanied us with a gesture signifying the opening of the A in the heart. Her joined fingers opened like a lotus. The sound emerged, grew, and gave birth to the U in the throat, which then blossomed into the resonance of the M in space. Devi had me observe the birds singing in the forest. She relaxed my throat with her fingers, delicately massaging my trachea.

"If you don't understand how the birds sing, the way in which the song makes them shudder and intoxicates them, you can't give life to the mantra. It's necessary to be entirely absorbed in the pleasure of the sound and let it rise naturally until the M becomes energy turning in the mouth, and the spirit of the sound climbs in its fullness to the bindu at the top of the skull. From this point on, the sound is no longer silence. It becomes radiance, spreading around you like a robe of pure light. Then it disperses into space and comes to germinate again in your heart. All energy is cyclical. Nothing is lost, nothing disappears, nothing is created. The mystical life is a spiral, a child's pinwheel upon which Shiva never stops blowing. You breathe; Shiva blows. You stop breathing; Shiva sleeps."

In *The Secret Music of the Soul*, Patrick Bernhardt describes the power of OM:

"In a comfortable position, let your body relax by breathing deeply. Once you are calm, pronounce the sacred mantra, without seeking reason on it but merely by trying, with a simple heart, to feel its exceptional frequencies. In a few minutes, all metaphysical explorations are forgotten and become useless since we penetrate into the unsuspected realm of mystical experience. Here is sound, vibrant with joy and impregnated with love. The heart expands under irradiating warmth. The mind which, a few minutes before, painfully spun in all directions is catapulted in a single direction, concentrated, focused on a point located at the center of the heart. A ray of peace illuminating the entire world, emanates from this point. Body and spirit are spontaneously bathed in an immense sense of gratitude. At one and the same time, we realize the power of the mantra and the stunning immensity of transcendental regions. He-who-does-not-dream, the awakened, the divine man can emerge from his old shell and can vibrate in harmony with the silent peace in which it is possible to perceive the sublime voice of his soul. When this hour comes, he knows that his dwelling is with the omniscience; he remembers that physical life is but a theatre performance. From this point on, he no longer fears anything."

"…all of creation is a result of vibration or Sound which slowly condenses and changes into material form. The Word differs from Sound in that it serves as a bridge between the Sound and the manifestation or creation.

"This bridge carries sound in two directions - out-going and in-going. The out-going Word changes to AUM. The in-going Word is the OM. The first Word, the AUM, differentiates into specific tones or notes and carries the purpose and the plan of the originator into manifestation. The second Word, the OM, is the bridge of Return which releases the Spirit from matter and leads it back Home, back to its Source…These two Words keep the manifestation of the Solar System in motion and form a way for cyclic manvantara and pralaya in all kingdoms. In a sense they are the yin and the yang within the wheel of Sound. Thus, the AUM expresses itself as the basic principle, energy, the fire which perpetuates existence. The OM is the pilgrim engaged in the process of leaving the not-self behind and climbing the ladder of evolution…

"To sum up, we can say that the AUM is the note of involution, creation and manifestation. It is a magical word which when adequately pronounced, brings the ideas and energies into objectification, materialization, or manifestation. The OM is used mostly for evolution, or let us say, spiritualization and liberation, for contact with the higher sources of energy and for unfoldment and blooming. Sound is the highest potency. It creates in out-breathing and annihilates in in-breathing."

From *Cosmos in Man*
Torkom Saraydarian

(Note: "Manvantara" and "Pralaya" are Sanskrit terms referring to the "days and nights" of a cycle of creation. Manvantara, the day, is the period of active manifestation (the out-breath) - the AUM described above. Pralaya, the night, refers to the period of dissolution or cosmic rest in between manifestation (the in-breath) - the OM)

"How must we sound the OM?

1. For the first OM the mind must be concentrated, but relaxed. The lips must form an ""O" and the full, round "O" sound must be sent forth. This "O" must rise as if you were pushing the sound to the roof of your mouth, on up to the middle of the top of your head, and out. As you are doing this, you must visualize your mental vehicle as becoming purer and more subtle.

2. The same visualization will be used for the second OM, but this time for the emotional body. Try to see the emotional body as a fine mist around you.

3. When sounding the third OM, relax the physical body completely, and imagine that your aura is becoming a golden color.

"The duration of the OM is divided into two parts, the 'O' and the 'M'. The sounding of the OM must be preceded by taking a deep breath. Its true effect starts after it has been sounded. We must allow an interval of silence as we end it, and in that short period of silence the effect of the OM enters deeper and deeper into the bodies. This effect can be compared to the effect of a stone thrown into a lake. Rings begin to form at the point where the stone enters the water, and continue to radiate outward long after the stone has sunk to the bottom. Similarly, in sounding the OM, a purifying influence spreads around us, and gradually rises to higher levels.

"When you feel any pressure in your head while chanting the OM, change the tone and note of your voice. This may help to remove the pressure. It will take a little time to find the correct note, the note which gives peace, clarity of mind and sensitivity to in-going energies.

"The time duration is important for both letters, O and M. Duration time of exhaling the breath in sound will be divided into two periods of ten or fifteen seconds for each letter, O-M. This time period, if filled with thoughts of the power of the OM when sounded, will form a strong foundation for future, advanced breathing.

"In this process, the note, the waves of sound or the vibration, does the cleaning, refining and expanding work for the vehicles and centers. The breath brings into these vehicles and centers the energy from the level on which you are focused in your consciousness."

From *Cosmos in Man*
Torkom Saraydarian

"The OM rightly sounded, releases the soul from the realm of glamour and of enchantment. It is the sound of liberation, the great note of resurrection and of the raising of humanity to the Secret Place of the Most High when all other Words and sounds have failed."

From *The Rays and the Initiations*
Alice A. Bailey

DIVINE CHANTS

"Chanting is how we enter into the eternal now. The energetic vibrations of our voices bond us to the spiritual light made of memory, and of now, and of future, for we are the light of universal intelligence. As we chant the Universe speaks to us in metaphoric images. Chanting calls the past and the future into the eternal now...When chanting or singing, the physical body experiences the essence of each word through the electricity, or light, created by Sound...

"Chanting contributes toward healing because it brings into alignment the physical, emotional, mental and spiritual bodies. It aligns them and integrates them into the here and now because past memory and future are healing as chanting is being done. With chanting the repeated sounds of the consonants direct the power of the vowels in such a way as to create an energy design...The vibratory essence of sound affects the inner walls of the nerves and blood vessels. The inner walls of each cell resonate and the power of vibration (sound) affects not only the physical cell walls but also the mental, emotional, spiritual walls."

From *Being and Vibration*
Joseph Rael

*W*hen words with specific meaning and intention are rhythmically sounded they are known as a "chant". Words hold vibrational resonance and sound acts as the wings upon which the consciousness of the words takes flight. As Joseph Rael in *Being and Vibration* puts it: "*…the importance in chanting is to become, through sound vibration, the essence of the word and thus to reach a level of ecstasy in which you realize a shift in consciousness.*"

The Logos, "the Creative Word" can be understood as an energetic means for structuring reality. In *The Rosicrucian Cosmos-Conception*, Max Heindel provides this description of the original manifestation of creation: "*The first aspect of the Supreme Being 'thinks out', or imagines, the Universe before the beginning of active manifestation, everything, including the millions of Solar Systems and the great creative Hierarchies which inhabit the Cosmic Planes of existence…The second aspect of the Supreme Being is that which manifests in matter as the forces of attraction and cohesion…This is 'The Word,' the 'creative fiat,' which molds the primordial Root-substance in a manner similar to the formation of figures by musical vibrations. So this great primordial 'Word' brought, or 'spoke,' into being, in finest matter, all the different Worlds, with all their myriad of Forms*".

Language gives birth to the forms of our ideas. In *The Book of Knowledge: The Keys of Enoch*, the "Living Language of Light" is described as the fiery, divine language which organizes harmonic patterns that quicken and align our minds with Universal God Consciousness. It refers to English as a "secondary language" that has lost touch with the original vibrational resonance still to be found in the root languages of Sanskrit, Egyptian, Tibetan, Chinese and Hebrew. "*These languages form a grid connecting the Higher I AM consciousness of Light with the human I AM consciousness of Light through a cosmic light vibration…the languages will open channels of crystalline vibration within you so that your body can work directly with the Higher Intelligence.*" These key languages are composed of sacred energy sounds. "*And when you use the divine names from all these five languages together, like Amen-Ptah - Egyptian, Phowa - Tibetan, Kuan-Yin - Chinese, Gabriel - Hebrew, and Buddha - Sanskrit, as mantra seed syllables, you set up a consciousness wavelength of light that resonates with all five bodies within you. Language, here, is a language of energy vibration formed by carefully selected seed mantras.*" (*The Book of Knowledge: The Keys of Enoch* by J. J. Hurtak).

Sanskrit, in particular, is considered by many Sanskrit scholars to be a "perfected language" of cosmic sound vibration that was constructed by the Devas to transmit divine information. It has been described as the "vibratory sound vibration of God" which communicates directly to the right brain.

The following collection of sacred healing mantras and chants are among my most loved. Many have been sung over the centuries and are imbued with a charged energy, a potent vibratory field that has accumulated with time and can be accessed via the mantra. They can be sung solo or in group ceremony. When chanting it is important to hold your intent, with your Third Eye and your Heart, on the specific energies you are invoking so that the energies can manifest through you. Rather than "making" the sound, the key is to allow oneself to become the vessel through which the sacred sound can flow.

ALOHA

This is the Huna mantra for love ~ the creative force of the Universe. The chanting of "AAAH - LOOOH - HAAA" opens the heart and connects you with the heart of the earth, the heart of God. It is a beautiful, simple chant that can be used to direct healing waves of love and peace around the world.

ELOHIM

Referred to in the Old Testament countless times, the Great Cosmic Elohim are known as the Master Builders of Creation or the collective Creative Godhead who brought the heavens and earth into form. The slow sounding of "EEEH - LOOOH - HEEEM" brings in a very holy energy and creates a vibratory field of sacred healing space.

SHEMA

Associated with both Atlantean and Kabbalah origins, this chant brings one into alignment with the feminine frequencies of God: love, unity, harmony, and the vibration of truth. "SHEEEE - MAAA". Described by *The Book of Knowledge: The Keys of Enoch*, *"Within the Kaballah, the sacred vibration of the 'Shema' is uttered for it carries with it the collective wisdom of the Masters to enable you to understand how your body can use thought-forms of the higher universe to be reunited with its higher Light body of creation."*

OM MANI PADME HUM

Over the centuries and to this day, throughout the mountains and villages of the Himalayas can be heard the beloved Sanskrit chant "OM - MAAAH - NEEEH - PAAAD - MEEEH - HUUUM" which means "Hail to the Jewel in the Lotus - to the God Within". Mani or jewel, refers to "enlightened compassion". Padme or lotus, symbolizes "wisdom". Hum is "that which nothing can disturb." It is a chant to the great Buddhist Bodhisattva, known as the Avalokiteshvara, who looks down with compassion on all living beings. This mantra connects one with the vibratory power of love, peace and compassion. It embodies a tremendous energy field that has been built through the wide and extensive usage of this chant.

"The most sacred of all the Eastern mantrams given out as yet to the public,
is the one embodied in the words: 'Om mani padme hum.'
Every syllable of this phrase has a secret potency, and its totality has
seven meanings and can bring about seven different results."

From *A Treatise on Cosmic Fire*
Alice A. Bailey

AMARUSHAYA

The name of the Angel of Divine Blessings. Invoking "AAAH - MAAA - RUUU - SHY - YAAA" brings the energies of love, healing and spiritual purpose to a ceremonial space. In *Angel Blessings*, Kimberly Marooney describes, *"Amarushaya builds the multidimensional structures that amplify and enhance the radiation of the blessing. You can feel the waves of energy she creates just by repeating the rhythm of her name several times - Amarushaya, Amarushaya, Amarushaya."*

ERI ERI

The hallowed name for Tane, the Hawaiian Heavenly Father. In *Children of the Rainbow*, Leinani Melville recounts that "EEER - REEE - EEER - REEE" was considered to be such a holy sound that only the Huna priests were allowed to use it in prayer. Leinani's description of Tane (Eri, Eri) provides a beautiful focus for this chant: *"...the fountainhead from whom the 'Water of Life' flowed. That 'Living Water' was the 'essence of spirit' or manna that coursed in His Holy Breath, pervaded all space and nourished all creatures with power to live by the Grace of God. He was the 'supporting root' that contained the essential spirit principle of life that caused the vine to develop in growth, expand and blossom."*

OM NAMAH SHIVAYA

When one listens to Guru Maya's beautiful version of this chant it is impossible to not feel a magical transformation occurring in the heart. The translation of this timeless Indian chant is: "I honour Shiva, the God Force which purifies my body and mind and awakens me to my inner self". "OM - NAAAH - MAAAH - SHEEE - VIII - YAAAH," especially when experienced in a group, creates a feeling of deep peace and solace which melts away outer concerns and envelops one in a blanket of serenity.

YOD HE VAV HE

"YOOOD - HEEEH - VAAAV - HEEEH" is the sacred name for God which is coded in our DNA, also known in the Kabbalistic tradition as the Tetragrammaton which is the Greek name for the four sacred letters (YHWH). From this holy "Name of Names" emanates the Ultimate Divine Vibration. It is the "word of light" that becomes life.

Described by philosopher and spiritual teacher, Omraam Mikahel Aivanhov, in *Angels and Other Mysteries of the Tree of Life*:

"The four letters of the name of God correspond to the four principles at work in the universe, and these four principles are also at work in human beings, for human beings were created in the image of the universe.

*"**Yod** is the creative masculine principle, the primordial force that is at the origin of all movement: the spirit, the father.*

*"**He** represents the feminine principle, which absorbs, preserves, protects, and allows the creative principle to work within her. This is the soul, the mother.*

*"**Vav** represents the son that is born of the union of the father and mother. It is the first-born of this union, and it, too, manifests itself as an active principle, although on a different level. The son is the intellect that follows the direction laid down by the father.*

*"The second **He** represents the daughter. The daughter is a repetition of the mother. This is the heart.*

"Thus the four letters of the name of God represent the father, the spirit; the mother, the soul; the son, the intellect, and the daughter, the heart."

William Gray, in *The Ladder of Lights* explains, *"In the old Qabalistic Tradition, the Divine Name was only passed on once in seven years from Master to disciple, 'mouth to ear'. At the Temple the High Priest alone was empowered to 'speak' the Name once a year when he entered the otherwise silent Holy of Holies which no other mortal might penetrate. Doubtless it was fully realized that the Tetragram used on such occasions was only a human substitute for the 'Lost Word' which if once recovered would restore Mankind to God-status. Possibly the sound of this conclusive Word is not unlike an atomic explosion."*

GAYATRI MANTRA

The Divine Mother of all mantras, the Gayatri mantra has been described as *"the key to opening the door of Cosmic Consciousness"* (Sadguru Sant Keshavadas).

"Gaya" means lifeforce and "tri" stands for protector, so the Gayatri is the protector of the lifeforce. Traditionally chanted at sunrise, noon and sunset, the Gayatri is acknowledged as the most potent, glorious and holiest of Vedic mantras, a sacred universal prayer that is practiced by Buddhists, Hindus and many others, transcending all religious boundaries with its original truth. Chanted in original Sanskrit, this song of protection, deliverance and divine wisdom purifies both the listener and the chanter.

"OM BHOOR BHUVAH SVAHA

TAT SAVITUR VARENYAM

BHARGO DEVASYA DHEEMAHI

DHIYO YO NAH PRACHODAYAAT"

The following is a breakdown of the Sanskrit meaning for each word:

OM - The Ultimate Reality

BHOOR - The Physical Earth

BHUVAH - Space, Ether, Mental Plane

SVAHA - Celestial Plane, Heaven, Causal Plane

TAT - "That" - The Essential Reality

SAVITUR - Radiant, Luminous, Enlightening Creative Sun

VARENYAM - To Adore and Worship

BHARGO - Permeated with Bliss and Luster

DEVASYA - Divine Grace

DHEEMAHI - To Contemplate, to Meditate

DHIYO - Intelligent Understanding

YO - Who

NAH - Us

PRACHODAYAT - Inspires, Enlightens

In *The Creative Fire*, Torkom Saraydarian provides this translation:

"OM

All of you, who are on earth,

Mid-world and Heaven

Let us meditate

Upon the Light adorable

Of the divine Sun of Life

To enlighten our souls."

One ancient version of the Gayatri is:

"Unveil to us the face of the true spiritual Sun,

hidden by a disk of golden light,

that we may know the truth and do our whole duty,

as we journey to Thy sacred Feet."

The Gayatri invokes the energy of the Sun (surya) and can be powerfully experienced when the chanter visualizes being bathed in a stream of magnetic light from the Great Central Sun and these rays being distributed around the world. As Torkom advises, "*When you repeat the Gayatri, especially in its Sanskrit form, you create a tremendous, unique vibration, a protective shield around you through which no low or hostile vibration can reach you. You can build this shield every time you repeat the Gayatri with great solemnity and joy.*" When I chant the Gayatri, I visualize myself being bathed with radiant waves of Divine Light which fill me with a feeling of immense well being, joyfulness and hope. I envision each cell in my body receiving an infusion of light and joining together to create a great flame of love. I link my flame with other heart flames around the world and this sea of flames enfolds the earth.

KADOSH, KADOSH, KADOSH,
ADONAI TSVAOT

"Holy, Holy, Holy is the Lord God of Hosts!"

Referred to in the scriptures of Revelation, this holiest of mantras is the song which resounds through the higher heavens. It holds an important key for our transformation. A song of divine attunement, it is said to tie the rhythms of our body together with the spiritual rhythms of our God Self and activates within us a sympathetic resonance with the Brother/Sisterhood of Light. The vibration of this mantra is so potent that negative forces cannot abide in its presence. I have found it extremely effective in clearing space of negative energies and have used it in healings with remarkable results. The use of "KAA DOH SH - KAA DOH SH - KAA DOH SH - AH DOH N'EYE - S'VAA OAT" sets up a resonance with Divine Love energies that cannot be accessed by lesser forces. It is the ultimate command for protection and claiming of sacred space.

SONG OF THE SOUL

Song of the Soul is a beautiful healing ceremony which incorporates toning and visualization. The recipient lies down, encircled by those who have gathered to perform the ceremony. The person is asked what name they would like to have sung: whether their given name or a special "spirit name". They can choose a specific colour in which to be bathed and a healing intention or personal affirmation they would like the group to hold for them. They may also request the singers to visualize a geometric shape around them, such as a pyramid or Merkaba. The group then begins (while holding the requested healing focus/colour/shape) softly whispering the name, slowly building to the melodic singing of it. The person receiving the Song of the Soul is thus bathed in a healing field of sound, colour and form.

There is something deeply moving about having your very Essence serenaded to; as though being recalled by your Divine Parents! Song of the Soul can be sung by mothers and fathers to their children to communicate how loved they are. When sung to the sick it provides a powerful healing transmission of love energy. It can also be used to aid in a soul's transition when it has chosen to leave the physical plane and move on to its next level of work.

The first time I received Song of the Soul was on my birthday at a sound healing workshop. It was performed outside in nature, the warm summer sun beaming down upon me while I was surrounded by a circle of over fifty human angels. As they sang, I was enfolded in a harmonic field of love energy and transported to higher realms.

"Sound, Star, and Light are all Inside."

Maharaj Sardar ahadur Jagat Singh

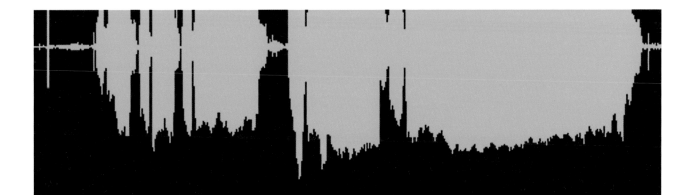

Harmonic Doorways

OVERTONES OF CREATION

"We are all overtones
of the Divine Violin String
and refractions of the Divine Light."

From *The Sacred Word and Its Creative Overtones*
Robert C. Lewis

*H*armonic overtones are a "stairway to heaven" of ascending and descending notes. They represent the harmonic principles upon which the Universe is structured. Overtones occur naturally within every sound, most of them beyond the range of our human ears. An overtone occurs when a fundamental note (whether played on a piano, cello or voiced) vibrates or "divides" itself into another note that resonates in a harmonic interval with the original tone. This first vibration continues to subdivide itself into a series of overtones, higher or lower, which can be heard simultaneously along with the fundamental tone. An infinite number of overtones can potentially be created from each fundamental note. From the fundamental note the first overtone vibrates at twice the rate of the first, the second overtone vibrates at three times the rate of the first and so on.

Hearing an overtone for the first time is magic, the second note seemingly appears from out of nowhere! Virtually anyone can learn to produce overtones through the toning of elongated vowel sounds by implementing slight variations in the way their mouth, lips and tongue are positioned as the sound emerges.

While overtone chanting has long been a part of ancient esoteric traditions around the world, David Hykes and The Harmonic Choir made it accessible to many in the modern world for the first time in 1975 with the fantastic recording *Hearing Solar Winds*. Listening to this, one is transported upon other-worldly harmonic sounds to new realms. The harmonics created through overtoning trigger a shift in our vibrational frequency and create a gateway through which we can travel the subtle fields of consciousness. Phenomenal shifts can be realized through the practice of singing overtone scales, finding a specific tone (such as the fifth octave up from the fundamental) and riding it for as long as possible. Within this elongated overtone, an opening or portal is created for voyage through the octaves of consciousness. In *Toward the One*, Hazrat Inayat Khan's son, Vilayat Inayat Khan provides this advice:

"Work with the sound until you are absolutely amazed that you could produce such a sound and it seems to you that you are just the instrument through which the divine pied piper blows the whisper of the incantations of his magical spell...

"Use the scale of overtones as a Jacob's ladder to climb. Jacob's ladder is like listening to the echo of an echo...

"Become yourself pure vibration beyond space. If the sound generated by the vocal chords into the vibratory network of the universe has the faculty of tuning one, it is because it links one with the cosmic symphony. The repetition of a physical sound sets off a sound current, a vibration tidal wave in the ether, by building up energy...

"We live on several planes at the same time. It is said in the Heikhaloth, the Jewish book of the heavenly spheres, that each time a new soul descends in the ocean of the manifested realm, it generates a vibration which is communicated to the entire cosmic ocean...Each creature is a crystallization of a part of this symphony of vibrations. Thus we are like a sound petrified in solid matter which continues indefinitely to resound in this matter and the word became flesh and the word became flesh and the word became flesh and...

"So you must become pure vibration and pass on through the other side."

"The Sacred Word and its Overtones will lead mankind

to the spiritual planes from which he came."

From *The Sacred Word and Its Creative Overtones*
Robert C. Lewis

Many of you probably had the experience of making overtone sounds as children although you may not remember it as such. Taking a deep breath, make the simple sound of UUU while puckering your lips as if blowing a kiss and moving your tongue slightly up and down within the cave of your mouth. Listen for variations in the sound as your tongue and lips slowly shift positions. At some point you will hear a different tone emerging on top of your original UUU. This is an overtone. Experiment by making the UUU sound in different notes; you may find a particular range of pitch (high or low) that is easiest for a harmonic to emerge.

Another combination to try is any two vowel sounds together, such as OU (as in who) and EEE. Slowly moving from OU to EEE with mouth puckered and the tongue curved slightly upward towards the roof of your mouth, you should experience raising overtones. Play with the position of your tongue and you will begin to detect a variation in tones being produced.

For a greater range of sounds, practice with MMM-OOO-AAH-EH-EEE-UUU-MMM moving very slowly form one vowel sound to the next. Listen closely for the overtones that appear as you slowly shift between the vowels. Practicing in the shower or a space with good acoustics will enhance your ability to hear the overtones you are producing.

The Mystery of the Seven Vowels by Joscelyn Godwin, declares *"The reawakened awareness of harmonics is perhaps the most significant musical development of the post-modern period, for it marks the re-establishment of music in its eternal and natural principles."* As we study the principles of harmonics more closely, we discover that they appear to be the very foundation upon which all creation was built.

"All of the vibrations that exist in the Cosmos are overtones of the fundamental tone of the Supreme Being. These overtones divide His ever existing, formless matter into all existing life, be it mineral life, plant life, animal or human life. This was brought about and is still being brought about by the crystallization of spirit into matter through a process of mutation, sympathetic vibration and magnetism. All of these processes are controlled by numerical relationships which are similar to the ratios between overtones in music." In this description from *The Sacred Word and Its Creative Overtones*, Robert C. Lewis explains how, from the original tone of Source, the overtones of creation were formed. He continues, *"All vibration is the result of uncountable trillions upon trillions of overtones emanating from other trillions upon trillions of overtones. All of these vibrations originally emanated from the fundamental tone of the Sacred Word."*

Delving further into the role played by overtones in the creative formation of the universe, an underlying theme of "seven" begins to emerge. *"It is on the number seven that Pythagoras composed his doctrine on the Harmony and Music of the Spheres. All the melody of nature is in those seven tones, and is therefore called 'the Voice of Nature'."*

These seven tones or "seven keys" are referred to throughout the esoteric mystery school teachings as well as traditional religions (Buddhist, Hindu, Egyptian, Jewish, Christian). The Seven Breaths of God, the Seven Rays, the Seven Great Logi, the Seven Spirits before the Throne of God, the Seven Creations, the Seven Solar Systems, the Seven Worlds, the Seven Laws, the Seven Conditions of Matter. The number seven is mentioned numerous times in Revelation. This structure of seven continually expresses itself throughout all the vibrations of creation, manifesting as the Seven Rays, the seven colours of the rainbow, the seven notes of the musical scale, the seven chakras, the seven days of the week, the seven vowels, the seven interlocking spheres which form the Seed of Life, referred to in The Emerald Tablets as a key to the secrets of knowledge.

"The Great Teacher teaches that all existence is a combination of musical notes.
Each plane, each dimension has its own note and sub-tones.
These forty-nine planes of Creation are seven octaves,
the various combinations of which are the Existence."

From *The Creative Sound*
Torkom Saraydarian

Commenting on the significance of seven, Robert C. Lewis adds that the Seven Great Logi *"…who could think whole solar systems and galaxies into existence with the powers delegated to them"* were the seven overtones which were *"emitted from the fundamental tone of the Supreme Being"*. He continues *"These seven great vibrations of spiritual thought project themselves through sympathetic vibration throughout all of creation. On the cosmic level they are the original overtones of the fundamental tone of the Supreme Being"*.

These seven original overtones are the seven streams or Seven Rays of creative energy from Source, the foundation behind all creation. They represent the materialization of spirit onto the physical plane that eventually returns to its Source. Once again Lewis explains,

"As the overtones proceed further and further away from the fundamental tone of the Supreme Being, the intervals between them become half steps, quarter steps, eighth steps. They become smaller and smaller on and on into infinity. One could speculate at this point that the intervals are so small that they are one with each other and resolve back to the whole, the fundamental tone of which they are a part.

All comes from God.

All exists in God.

All goes back to God.

From the Infinite --------To the Infinite."

HEALING WITH HARMONICS

*I*f overtones are indeed the vibrational building blocks of creation, clearly they hold a vital key for our return to wholeness. One extraordinary healing technique utilizes the alchemy of harmonics to retune our energy fields. This involves scanning the body using harmonic overtones and, with hands cupped around the mouth to focus the sound, directing these overtones to specific areas where imbalance exists. In dolphin-like fashion, one is using the voice as a sonic sensor and feedback device to locate the imbalance. As the harmonics resonate with the energies of a specific center, discordant frequencies are reharmonized.

Receiving an attunement through vocal overtoning can have a profound impact as the body is seemingly transformed into a human tuning fork. This type of sound therapy requires a high level of sensitivity on the part of the practitioner who, in an intimate way, is using his or her sacred breath and sound as an instrument to merge with the energy field of another. It is essential that one become an empty vessel or hollow reed, allowing the breath to flow without human interference so the needed tones can emerge. There is no formula for this technique, no perfect note to hit. Call in your higher guidance…allow your voice to find the vowel sound and note that feels right and ride that sound for as long as you feel the energy shifting. Your intuition will tell you when it is time to change to another note and when to move to another part of the body. Most people have never felt sound move through their body in this way. It can have a deep aligning effect. A ten minute period of silence to assimilate the energies after this sound treatment is essential.

HARMONIC UNION

*P*erhaps the ultimate sound experience occurs when two individuals join to create sacred harmonics. Linking their intent, a connection is made between their Third Eye, Heart and Throat centers. Standing or sitting in close range to one another so that their sounds can resonate, two can create harmonic overtones which merge together and form additional overtones. As each one's harmonics dance with the other's, a new harmonic of sound emerges from the ethers. Through this union of overtones, a heavenly melting into oneness is experienced; a divine sound fusion.

If this exercise is done with a love partner, it can be practiced as a sacred sound tantra. With both partners' lips touching and mouths open to allow the sound to flow through, a joint resonance chamber or sound cave is formed in which their overtones meet and coalesce, forming a third level of harmonics. This sound kiss is an extremely intimate and powerful act of sound creation which reverberates throughout both bodies simultaneously. With a focused healing intent, you can direct these overtones inward through your beloved's energy centers. Our bodies love to be sung to!

Harmonic overtoning incorporated into lovemaking balances not only the energy fields of both partners, its vibrational waves spiral outward to impact the whole of the cosmos. Sacred ceremonial unions performed with this level of conscious intention, have enormous healing potential.

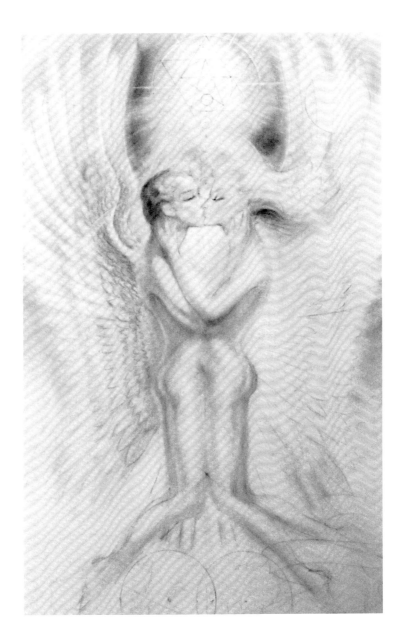

"The primary tone,
the foundation stone of all worlds,
is sung by the quartz crystal."

From *Voices of Our Ancestors*
Dhyani Ywahoo

CRYSTAL SOUND

Liquid Crystalline Substance

Beautiful harmonic overtones are generated when quartz crystal singing bowls are played. The sound produced by crystal bowls is rich in harmonics, making them valuable vibrational healing tools. Traditional Cherokee teachings describe quartz crystal as the greatest of healers.

"The sound structure of the crystal resonates, recalling to its optimum resonance and pitch the sound within yourself, the note of your perfection. The crystal is a tuning fork, ever resonating the sound of Creation within each being."

From *Voices of Our Ancestors*
Dhayani Ywahoo

From a scientific viewpoint, quartz crystal is a mixture of the elements silicon and oxygen that take on hexagonal forms. Quartz contains the property of piezoelectricity, which means it has the ability to produce a programmable electrical impulse. It can receive, store, amplify and transmit information, which is why it is a key component in watches, radio, television and computer chips.

"Quartz is the stepped down crystallization of the White Light spectrum...
"Quartz has few peers in its renowned capacity to receptively imprint vibrational energy patterns and to maintain such informational coding steady within its latticework with virtual permanence."

From *The Crystal Connection*
Randall Baer & Vikki Baer

Quartz crystal also responds to the electrical impulses produced by our body and our thoughts, and naturally resonates with the crystalline substance that exists in our DNA, bones, blood and body fluids. We are composed of crystal! We, therefore, have a natural built-in attunement with crystal bowls; our bodies are natural crystal resonance chambers.

While similar in concept to the ancient singing bowls of Tibet, vibrationally there is a significant difference. Tibetan bowls are traditionally composed of seven different metals that possess a denser, earth bound energy. Crystal bowls are composed of pure, crushed, powdered quartz crystal that is spun at high speed, ignited with an electric arc torch and fused together to form a bowl. Their crystalline quartz nature embodies pure light vibration that resonates with our etheric light bodies, making them a perfect tool for programming and transmitting specific healing intentions.

Crystal sound is a tremendous purifier. It bathes the body in luminous light.

INITIATION

*T*he first time I heard a crystal singing bowl was over the telephone. The vibration travelled through the receiver into my right ear and instantaneously into every atom in my body. I felt an electrical energy surge through every cell as the tone propelled me into a heightened state of consciousness. While not everyone has this dramatic a reaction, for me it was an indication of my future work with crystal sound. Within a week I had ordered a complete chakra tuned set of seven bowls and my work with the crystal bowls began in earnest. Even before opening their shipping boxes, I could sense the Spirit of the bowls filling my meditation room. "They" had arrived to initiate my work with crystal sound and so began my experience…

Fortunately I had no formal training in working with the crystal bowls and so I was able to discover for myself the immense gifts they bring. What we learn through our own practice becomes integrated within us.

The crystal bowls are simple to play and require no special musical ability. They are instruments of tone and vibration and are played by rotating a rubber ball mallet around the outer or inner circumference of the bowl. By varying the pressure and speed of the mallet, you can achieve a softer or fuller tone. When playing crystal bowls, louder is not better. Crystal sound is a powerful medicine with a penetrating ability to reach us in our deepest places. As their sound waves permeate our various bodies (physical, emotional, mental, spiritual) energies are stirred and old blocks or crystalizations may be dislodged and freed.

CRYSTAL BOWL SPECIFICS

*E*ach bowl, depending on its size and the width of its walls, sings at a specific frequency and note. Bowls range in size from 5 1/2 inch to the great temple bowls of 20, 22 and 24 inch circumferences. Most notes are available in most size ranges. A 10 inch B note will be a higher pitch while an 18 inch B will sing with a deeper, lower resonance. The optically clear bowls play with a very sweet, bell-like tone. They go through the firing process three times to achieve their clarity. They are lighter in weight and suited for playing on the Third Eye, Crown or Throat chakras where the weight of larger, frosted bowls would be uncomfortable. They emit a penetrating, laser-like focus. Frosted bowls are the most popular and versatile. 12, 13 and 14 inch bowls are excellent all purpose ones, light and easily portable. The 16, 18 and 20 inch bowls sing with a deeper, longer lasting resonance and much more vibrational power. They are wonderful played directly on the body, especially along the back of the spine which functions as a dynamic sound resonator, distributing sound vibration throughout the body.

INNER BODY SOUND MASSAGE

*I*t is one level of experience to hear a recording of crystal bowls, another to be present in a room while they are being played live, and yet another to experience them played directly on your body. The latter provides a profound experience of sound merging with your body. All outside distraction disappears as your attention is focused and you become one with the tone. This "inner body sound massage" functions like a divine tuning fork, bringing us back into a state of harmony and attunement.

An effective way to demonstrate this process is by using a crystal bowl to make "structured water" which organizes the water's molecules into a crystalline pattern; a very healthful water to drink. I fill up a 12, 13 or 14 inch bowl close to half full with water (an A or B note is my preferred for this purpose) and proceed to play. At first a herring-bone pattern forms on the water's surface, then effervescent bubbles begin to well up and finally, when I reach a certain speed and pressure with the mallet, the water begins to dance up out of the bowl in a cascading fountain, forming a beautiful, symmetrical pattern. This provides a very visual source for understanding the power of sound to move matter. Our bodies are composed of approximately 80% water, making them a perfect conduit for sound, as sound waves travel close to five times faster through water than air. In the same way that the sound arranges the water in the bowl, so does it organize the water and crystalline components of the tissues, cells, and organs of our body into a harmonious, tuned formation. The power of this sound magic is grounded in the law of physics!

One of the beautiful aspects of working with crystal bowl medicine is that it does not require a leap of consciousness on the part of the recipient to benefit from the treatment. A person receives whatever they need from the sound from the level they are ready to receive. From a purely physical perspective, the relaxing alpha tones produced by the bowls can lower heart rate, respiration, and blood pressure. On an emotional level, they reduce stress and have a definite calming effect. On the mental level, they calm the cluttered mind and bring clarity. On a spiritual level, they open gateways to expanded consciousness and can facilitate shamanic travel into other dimensions.

Playing the crystal bowls led me naturally into toning along with their sounds. Here I discovered a powerful fusion between the external sound of the bowl and the self-generated sound of my voice. I have found that by having my mouth in close proximity to the bowl as I am playing (sitting cross-legged on the floor and bending my mouth toward the bowl)… a sweet spot appears where the tone of my voice merges perfectly with the tone of the bowl. At this point I can feel the harmonics of the bowl and my voice interplay with one another and a fluid, river of sound flows forth.

WORKING WITH DIFFERENT MUSICAL SYSTEMS

The most widely used system today that relates musical notes to the body's chakra centers, has Ayurvedic origins:

CHAKRA	NOTE
Crown	B
Third Eye	A
Throat	G
Heart	F
Solar Plexus	E
Sacral	D
Root	C

There is another system that is Taoist in origin, based on a series of fifth intervals (moving upward from the Root center, F to C is a fifth interval, C to G, G to D, etc.):

CHAKRA	NOTE
Crown	B
Third Eye	E
Throat	A
Heart	D
Solar Plexus	G
Sacral	C
Root	F

I have used both systems with equal effectiveness. The nature of the human mind is such that we love to follow a system but this can be limiting. My experience has been that one day my body may respond in the heart region to the note of D while on another it may resonate with the note of F or C or B. Our body drinks in the tone and frequency it needs in the moment. Above all we need to work simply with our intuition. While you can use the standard chakra system of notes with excellent results, do not be bound by it. It may in fact be the frequency of B that your Solar Plexus needs to help move that block of fear, not the E that is normally associated with it. Everybody is unique, everyone resonates to his or her own tones and this continues to change as we shift our frequency. There are no formulas that will work all the time; the single most important factor is the intent you hold while making the sound.

CRYSTAL BOWL MEDITATION

A single crystal bowl is a valuable instrument for personal meditation. With a bowl resting upon my lap, my hands gently cupping the sides of the bowl, I begin in silence. As I hold this pure crystal vessel, I empty my mind of external thoughts and desires and become a chalice, tuning to the divine love and wisdom of my God Presence. I visualize my body as a crystal cup, a container that is being filled with the blazing white fire of purity and I enter the sacred sanctuary of my heart.

After this period of silent prayer, I begin to play the bowl by lightly tapping the outer rim of the bowl and then slowly working the sound into a continual spiraling tone. I work directionally with the mallet depending on how I wish to work with the sound. By playing the bowl in a counterclockwise fashion, I hold the intent of travelling deeper within my Self; connecting with the core of my essence (yin). When playing the bowl clockwise (yang) I direct the energies into outer manifestation. An example would be if I wish to send healing currents to someone long distance or to encompass the entire world in a rose pink flame of Divine Love. A further distinction can be made by playing the bowl on either the top inside rim or outside rim. The sound created by playing the bowl on the inside is a softer, gentler, more yin energy while playing the outer rim produces a louder, stronger vibration.

A simple and beautiful way to create a sacred space for meditation in the evening hours is to place a pillar style candle in the center of a bowl. Gazing into a crystal bowl with a candle burning from within is a powerful focusing meditation. I use pure beeswax candles that I make in the spectrum of rainbow colours. You can work with the colours of the chakras, choosing the appropriate colour/note to identify each bowl. With no artificial light, the flame of the coloured candles glows through the frosted quartz bowls casting a beautiful, soft light for your ceremonial and healing work.

Vibrationally you are working with colour and sound. You can also add the element of aromatherapy by rubbing some essential oil on the inside of the bowl, the warmth of the candle flame will send gentle wafts of fragrant essence into the air. Another meditative way to play with a crystal bowl is with the element of water in a bathtub. Any bowl will easily float with one hand underneath to gently hold it in place. The sound waves from the bowl travel effortlessly through the water and anyone in it. A deeply cleansing and purifying experience that is highly recommended!

HARMONIC INTERVALS

With multiple crystal bowls you can create harmonic intervals which affect the energy body and provide gateways for cosmic energies. For example a C bowl played in conjunction with an E bowl creates a major third interval (used often by Bach) which invokes a joyful response in our emotional body. An A bowl played with a C, creates a minor third interval which produces the sad, love-angst tone prevalent in country music.

Fifth intervals are extremely healing combinations. The C bowl with a G bowl creates a fifth. You don't need much of a musical background to work with this. By simply counting along any five notes of the seven note musical scale, A B C D E F G, you will have a fifth interval combination. (So A and E make a fifth, as do B and F, as do C and G, D and A (of the next octave), E and B (of the next octave), F and C (of the next octave), and G and D (of the next octave). Understanding this, you will see how the Taoist based system (which relates F to the Root, C to the Sacral, G to the Solar Plexus, D to the Heart, A to the Throat, E to the Third Eye and B to the Crown) follows a series of fifth intervals. The energy of the fifth is very freeing and clean, it carries us beyond any emotional stickiness to a place of creative openness. Rudolph Steiner described the experience of the fifth as *an expansion into the vast Universe*. I like to play a 16 inch G on the mid to upper back area while at the same time playing a 14 inch C balanced above the knees on the upper thighs. This fifth interval combination of C with G produces a very calming, soothing effect on the nervous system.

Playing with octaves is another wonderful combination to explore. The sound of the octave created by playing a 10 inch B bowl by the Crown chakra along with an 18 or 20 inch B over the Solar Plexus has an energy of completeness. The whole body seems to stretch into the Greater Body it is a part of. To create harmonies such as these, you need compatible bowls. Playing a C bowl that is slightly sharp with an E that is slightly flat, will sound off. Working with a tuned chakra set means that the bowls are in pitch and harmonious.

CHAKRA TUNED SETS

For those interested in exploring the world of crystal sound in depth, a chakra tuned set offers a wide range of possibilities. I like to arrange my set of bowls in a large circle on the floor and sit in the middle where I can easily pivot around the circle. Organizing them in a circle of fifths (so that the bowls adjacent to each other produce a fifth interval when played together) allows me to move clockwise around the circle and play a continual spiral of fifths.

Working with a chakra set provides a powerful sound therapy that can complement many healing practices. Widely used by healing touch and reiki practitioners, yoga instructors and massage therapists, crystal bowl applications are limited only by one's imagination. One of the most potent ways to utilize the full healing capabilities of a chakra tuned set is through the experience of an energy attunement…

ENERGY ATTUNEMENTS

"The process of healing involves tuning our bodies to our inner Core, and then to the Cosmic note of the Central Core of the Universe."

From *New Dimensions in Healing*
Torkom Saraydarian

Crystal bowl attunements provide a vibrational inner alignment, harmonizing us with both our inner Core and that of the Universe. A full session requires at least an hour and a half. I begin with a prayer invoking the flow of Divine healing energies to be directed for the person's highest good and in accordance with their Higher Self. I usually start with the person lying on their back while I play a 10 or 12 inch B bowl, supported by my hand and resting gently on the top of their head at the Crown Chakra. The bowl functions as a receiving vessel and distributor of the luminous currents of Sound and Light flowing in from the higher centers. At this point many people feel as though they are floating on a river of sound. The Crown is associated with the 1st Ray of Divine Will and the sacred center of Shamballa.

Over the Third Eye I place a clear, 8, 9 or 10 inch bowl; an A or E depending on the system I have chosen to work with. These clear bowls are lighter in weight than the frosted bowls and their clarity is well suited for working with this energy center. The Third Eye is key for penetrating the veils which may be clouding one's higher vision and for aligning one's personal will with Divine Will.

Moving down to the Throat Chakra I again use a small, clear bowl in either a G or A. The Throat is the center for creative self expression and speaking our truth. It is a channel for the Third Ray energies of Creative Intelligence.

Over the Heart I play a frosted F or D in any range from a 10 to a 16 inch depending on the size of the person and my intuitive feel for the tone required; the smaller bowls playing a higher, sweet tone; the larger bowls a deeper, full tone. The Heart Center is associated with the 2nd Ray of Love/Wisdom and connects us with the Heart of the Christ.

Moving to the Solar Plexus I choose from a 12 to 18 inch E or G or, depending on the work we are doing, I may decide to place one of the great 20, 22 or even 24 inch bowls over a larger area encompassing both the Solar Plexus and the Sacral areas. These larger bowls are usually only available in A, B, C and D notes. It should be noted here that each crystal bowl has its own unique energy that one needs to be familiar with in order to intuit where it would be most useful. An example of this is my 24 inch B bowl. The tone it produces is low and deep, soothing and calming. Played over the Solar Plexus it has the effect of assisting a person in riding the spiral of sound to their very central core and experiencing a place within themselves which is beyond fear and emotional stress…the feeling of the Soul being cradled and soothed in the very loving, compassionate arms of the Divine Mother. At this point many people want to continue with this bowl for a longer period of time because it transports them to such a deep, sacred space within. In contrast to this energy, my 24 inch C bowl has a very grounding physical influence. It has an energizing effect on the body and is useful when strengthening of the physical vehicle is called for. You stay very present with this bowl while the B tends to transport one into other realms.

When ready, I continue to move down the body over the Sacral area with a 10, 12, 13, 14, 15 or 16 inch D or C bowl. For the Root Chakra, I will play a C or F on the thighs just above the knees or lower on the legs just below the knees. Once again the size of the bowl played is intuited, dependent upon a person's body weight and the tone required. At this point I have the person flip over onto their tummy and I begin by playing a bowl on the soles of their feet. Propping a pillow under their feet helps to support the feet in the proper position. Experiment with the size of bowl that plays best. Moving up along the legs, an important spot connected with the heart is over the back of the knees. Then working my way up to the lower spine, mid spine, upper spine, shoulders, back of the neck where the "Mouth of God" or Zeal Point resides, then finally to the back, top of the head and the area where we began.

Once the body has been tuned and is deeply relaxed from the crystal bowls, harmonic overtoning and the use of otto tuners can provide a deep and very focused final tuning. Otto tuners are tuning forks whose end tip makes contact with the body, delivering a soft, pulsing vibration of frequency to specific areas, such as the key meridian points. This "laser light tool" directs a very precise, focused beam of frequency which the body (prepared for by the crystal bowls) feels with heightened sensitivity, providing a finishing touch to the attunement.

This overview is provided as an example only, it is certainly not a formula for every attunement. Every healing is unique and must be intuitively tailored to the individual. It is vital to elicit feedback from the person receiving the attunement in terms of how they are feeling; if a bowl feels uncomfortable in a certain area or won't play, these are clear signs to use an alternative. One of the positive aspects of working with the bowls is that they enable us to access doorways of our consciousness while remaining present in our body. They assist us in integrating the higher energies into our body rather than floating off into the ethereal, thus I rarely encounter grounding problems at the end of a session. Most people are very alert, energized and in their bodies in a fuller way than they may ever before have experienced. It is sometimes difficult to bring the session to a close because it just feels so good! As mentioned previously, it is also extremely important to allow for a period of silence after the sound during which one can integrate the healing energies. After the external sound has stopped, the sound continues to echo within our body chamber.

CLEANSING CRYSTAL BOWLS

*C*rystal is an extremely efficient holder and transmitter of energies and it is vital to keep crystal bowls clear and purified. This is especially true after they have been used in a healing. On the physical level, a soak in water (preferrably salt) is the most thorough method. For any hard to clean stains, a paste of baking soda on a toothbrush works well. Rinse and dry carefully. An essential oil mixed with water can be spritzed on the bowl - juniper is very purifying. Other methods include smudging with sage or cedar or using a specific tuning fork known as a crystal tuner which emits a frequency of 2675 (said to be the frequency of quartz crystal). Lightly tap the tuning fork on a piece of wood and encircle the bowl, allowing the sound waves to wash over it.

As well as any of the above methods, I always invoke the Sacred Violet Flame to cleanse and purify. Crystal is a living consciousness that appreciates the care it is given. My crystal bowls love being out in the natural elements: they enjoy a refreshing, cleansing rain; they are recharged with solar energies when set out for a sun bath; they also love to spend the night outside to soak up the revitalizing energies of the stars and the full moon.

CIRCLE OF FIFTHS

*A*nother application of the crystal bowls involves working with musical chords and the specific qualities they embody. Over the years I have added to the original seven notes of my chakra set C, D, E, F, G, A, B, - the five sharps (the black notes on a piano) of A#, C#, D#, F#, G#. This twelve note combination forms the chromatic musical scale in crystal bowls which I arrange in a circle, in a wheel of fifth intervals. With either the player or another positioned in the center of this configuration, different musical chords can be played to provide a sound bath of healing harmonies.

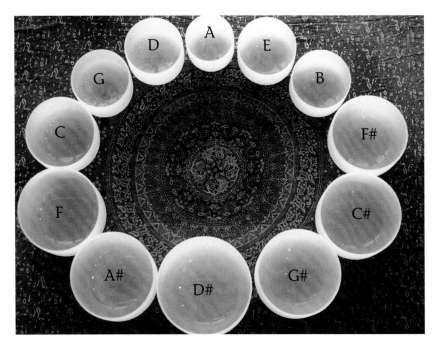

In his book *Aura-Shield of Protection & Glory*, Torkom Saraydarian explains, *"The Solar Lord is playing His music on twelve planetary notes. The goal of each person is to make that solar music echo in his own tiny aura and find creative expression through it, until 'as above, so below' is realized and actualized...Eventually the aura becomes a wheel of twelve spokes which revolve at such an incredible speed that it appears as if the wheel is standing still, and all twelve rays are clearly seen. This stage is the stage of glory, or we say that the person now wears the Robe of Glory."*

He provides the following chord association for each zodiacal sign:

ZODIAC SIGN	CHORD	PRIMARY COLOUR	KEYNOTE
ARIES	**C** E G	Red	Courage, strength
TAURUS	**C#** F G#	Red-Orange	Patience
GEMINI	**D** F# A	Orange	Transmutation of fear
CANCER	**D#** G A#	Orange-Yellow	Joy, enthusiasm
LEO	**E** G# B	Yellow	Purification
VIRGO	**F** A C	Yellow-Green	Power
LIBRA	**F#** A# C#	Green	Integration with nature
SCORPIO	**G** B D	Green-Blue	Revitalization
SAGITTARIUS	**G#** C D#	Blue	Unity, devotion
CAPRICORN	**A** C# E	Blue-Violet	Regeneration
AQUARIUS	**A#** D F	Violet	Brotherhood
PISCES	**B** D# F#	Violet-Red	Understanding

NOTE: The first note (in bold) of each chord is the primary note associated with the zodiacal sign and the note to which the primary colour corresponds.

One way of working with this wheel is to begin by playing the key chord of one's sun or one's rising sign while repeating the sacred OM seven times, once for each of the seven spheres of our subtle bodies (Atmic, Buddhic, Causal, Mental, Astral, Etheric, Physical). Then all twelve planetary chords can be sounded to balance and attune with the energies of the great wheel of solar music. As well, every month specific astrological energies exert a key influence on all of us and it is beneficial to work with the zodiac chords of the specific month, especially at the time of the full moon when we are showered with heightened frequencies.

CEREMONIES OF SOUND AND LIGHT

The first time I entered the Star Dome of the Vancouver Planetarium, I felt as though I was standing beneath a giant, upside down crystal bowl. I knew instinctively that this "sound chamber of stars" would be a magical space in which to hold crystal bowl ceremonies. It has since become the site for several Sound and Light Ceremonies, celebrating the key turning points of the equinoxes and solstices during which a great flood of heightened energies and cosmic forces pour onto earth. These concerts weave a dance of sound and light with live crystal bowl music, drumming, toning and chanting, together with the sensation of travelling amid the movement of the stars, the orbit of the planets, and the spinning galaxies of space. This provides an audible and visual journey to the depths of one's inner space as well as outer.

The sound vibration created when a group of two hundred people seated within the circular dome begin to tone "OM" is tremendous. It travels in a spiral motion and you can physically feel this sound wave move through your body as it rotates around the circle. This carrier wave of sound generates a unified force field through which the higher energies can be absorbed and distributed.

It has been said that peace will return to earth when ceremonial attunement to the Cosmos is kept once again. Ceremonies such as these provide those gathered with a great downpouring of higher frequencies. The Great Ones use these opportunities to expand our consciousness, to assist us in aligning our personal will with Divine Will, and to impulse our striving towards world unity and service.

NATURE'S SOUND TEMPLES

Crystal bowls have a special affinity for being played outdoors. Living on an island on the West Coast of British Columbia, I am fortunate to live in close proximity with nature. I often take some of my smaller bowls on wilderness field trips (wrapped in blankets in a backpack) and play them in many of the area's magical spots: on a sandy beach by the ocean shore where their tones serenade the sea elementals; in the forest while playing to the tree spirit of a mighty pine; on the top of a mountain toning to the magnificent nature devas of the mountain.

"High mountains send out healing radiations for a 50-mile radius. The snow upon the mountains giveth a purifying element. When the disciple standeth within the 50-mile radius, he receiveth the healing radiation from the mountain, and he carrieth it beyond the radius of the mountain. This radiation moveth from the disciple into the luminous bodies of other men, giving peace."

From *The Venerable One*
Ann Ree Colton

At the base of one mountain I discovered a cave which tunnels over 200 feet into the earth. The path into the cave veers and twists, leading to a small alcove at the end. Within this inner retreat of solid rock and earth, no outside noise penetrates. It provides an incredible resonance chamber for sound. The first time I entered this cave accompanied by a friend, I had a remarkable experience with what is termed "acousto-luminesence" - the ability of soundwaves to be converted into lightwaves. I had read of this phenomenon but never experienced it myself. As we made our way into the cave, the light faded and we could no longer see where we were going. I paused and took a small clear crystal G bowl out of my pack and began to play it while overtoning the OM. A soft, diffused light appeared which we assumed was coming from a hole in the ceiling of the cave. Walking further in, we discovered there was no such opening, yet the cave was undeniably lighter!

116

Reaching the end of the chamber, we lit some candles and played the crystal bowl and a drum. The cave's curved rock walls provided magnificent sound amplification. The acoustics in this natural sound chamber were incredible! Sitting deep within the inner chambers of Her body, I felt completely at one with the Mother. As the crystal sound waves echoed through the earth's veins, I could feel the consciousness of the crystal merging with the quartz crystal kingdom. Enfolded in this womb of earth, sound and crystal, a deep comfort descended.

I have since returned with small groups to this resonance chamber, conducting sound ceremonies with crystal bowls, gongs, tuning forks, toning and chanting. With candles nestled into rock crevices at various levels, this sacred cave becomes aglow, transformed into a luminous cathedral of sound and light or "flaming sound". Amid the pure beauty of nature's temples, we are guided to the stillness of the temple residing in our hearts, where the cave of love is revealed.

WHEEL OF THE SEVEN RAYS CEREMONY

FOR PERSONAL AND PLANETARY HEALING

The crystal bowls are natural instruments for use in sacred ceremony. Their continual, elongated tone provides a perfect accompaniment to chanting. They can be played individually or two harmonious bowls simultaneously to create a vibrational background for silent meditation.

A group ceremonial wheel representing the Seven Rays of Creation can be formed with a seven note chakra set arranged in a circle. The circle provides a container for the energies. This ceremony can be conducted to activate our Light Body and for the purification and healing of ourselves and the earth as we anchor in the divine qualities of the Rays. It is especially potent when performed during the time of the full moon, when transmission of the Ray energies is at a peak.

"Sound initially radiated seven energy currents which are called the Seven Rays. Each Ray is a note. Each note, or Ray, creates a plan. We are told that the continuity of sound brought into existence seven Cosmic Planes. Each Plane is becoming an octave with seven notes. The human being in his own form is an embodiment of seven and forty-nine notes."

From *The Creative Sound*
Torkom Saraydarian

In this ceremony, each one of seven crystal bowls is designated to represent one of the Seven Ray energies. Seven people each chose a specific bowl and take their places around the circle. Each is responsible for holding the focus of their particular bowl's Ray energy in the wheel. Beginning with the 1st Ray, moving around the circle in a clockwise direction, one by one the individual bowls are played and the divine qualities of each Ray invoked. The energies of each Ray are directed into the center of the wheel, weaving a beautiful vortex, a spiral of cascading colours which bathes the ceremonial space and all its participants. This energy then expands outward on the carrier wave of sound and light that has been created to form harmonic gridworks of love and unity around the earth.

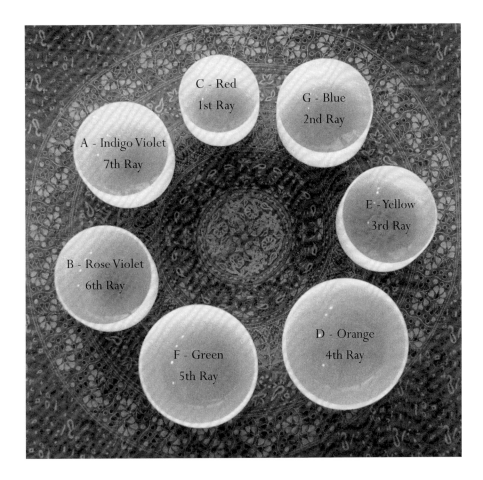

C - Red
1st Ray

G - Blue
2nd Ray

A - Indigo Violet
7th Ray

E - Yellow
3rd Ray

B - Rose Violet
6th Ray

D - Orange
4th Ray

F - Green
5th Ray

NOTE: The complex nature of the Cosmic Rays is expressed as octaves of sound and colour interweaving through the spheres of the manifested universe. There are numerous levels of expression and varied musical note/colour/Ray correlations that one may research. The colour/Ray association used in this ceremony is based on teachings referred to in *Aura - Shield of Protection and Glory* by Torkom Saraydarian as well as those intuited by the author.

This ceremony offers keys for tuning to the Seven Great Rays of Creation which emanate throughout space and pervade all kingdoms of life. The Seven Rays are the great builders; the creative forces behind all manifestation. Each Ray is a fiery stream of energy that embodies specific qualities of the Divine Nature. Working with their potent, magnetic radiations initiates an expansion of consciousness, stimulates a process of purification within us, and calls our soul's highest potential to unfold in our life.

We begin by opening our heart to the unified field of love and focusing our awareness inward as we invoke the Divine Universal Light to enfold us with pure Source vibration. As these streaming, crystalline Rays of Sound and Light cascade through our body, we become a conduit for their luminous energies, radiating to the inner sun within us. Breathing deeply, absorb these charged atoms of light into every cell as you ground with Mother Earth. Intend to receive the highest possible for you at this time.

We invoke the presence of the Great Ones Who oversee the pouring forth of the Seven Rays of Creation from the Highest Realms. These Divine Emanations stream through the Cosmic Planes, bathing us with their fundamental tones, their primordial vibrations of creation.

Representative for 1st Ray begins playing C bowl:

We call to the 1st Ray of Divine Will to shower us with your tones of Red and the Power and the Spirit of The Father.

You provide us with strength, purpose and the power to initiate new action. You are the creative force of birth as well as the destruction of limitations. You are the force of unity and synthesis. Through you we are connected with the Divine Plan and the sacred center of Shamballa. As your energies flow through our Crown , we align with God's Will.

May your energies gently rotate around us in a spiraling, clockwise circle.

Representative for 2nd Ray begins playing G bowl:

We call forth the 2nd Ray of Love and Wisdom to bathe us with your tones of Blue and your consciousness of Eternal Love and Light.

You are the Cosmic magnetic love force (The Sun/Son) that binds together Spirit and Matter. You are the attraction of the Light. You carry the unifying energies of compassion, healing and world teaching. As you flow through our Heart, we are connected to the Heart of the Cosmic Christ and the Great Brother/Sisterhood of Light.

May your energies join in spiraling harmony with those of the 1st Ray.

Representative for 3rd Ray begins playing E bowl:

We call forth the 3rd Ray of Active Creative Intelligence to infuse us with your tones of Yellow and your substance of Intelligent Matter, The Mother.

You are the Great Architect of the Universe. You are the organization of thought shaping atoms into form. You are the stimulation of clear mental ideas. You assist us in actualizing and manifesting plans. As you flow through our Throat center, you evoke the power of clear communication.

May your frequencies weave into the swirling spiral of tones and colours.

Representative for the 4th Ray begins to play D bowl:

We call the 4th Ray of Harmony and Beauty to radiate your tones of Orange and your energies of Peace and Balance.

You are The Great Bridge. You are the harmonization of discord. You carry the design of beauty and art, colour and sound. You are sensitivity and intuition. You evoke understanding and the overcoming of dissonance.

May your vibrations blend in harmony with the other circling Rays.

Representative for the 5th Ray begins to play F bowl:

We call the energies of the 5th Ray of Knowledge and Concrete Science to imbue us with your frequencies of Green and Divine Knowledge.

You are the scientific mind of discoveries; the development of ideas and tangible knowledge. You are the Laws of

Nature and the Revealer of Truth. You embody the qualities of courage and striving.

May your energies join in the orbiting sphere of vibrations.

Representative for the 6th Ray begins to play B bowl:

We call the 6th Ray of Devotion and Idealism to bathe us with your tones of Rose Violet and your essence of pure Devotional Love.

You are the ideal that inspires us to evolve. You are fiery enthusiasm and spiritual aspiration. You are the nature of faith, loyalty and service.

May your energies unite with the cascading currents of Rays.

Representative for the 7th Ray begins to play A bowl:

We call forth the 7th Ray of Ceremonial Magic to transmit your radiations of Indigo Violet and your Sacred Flame of Initiation.

You are the magical work of the Soul that fuses spirit and matter, masculine and feminine. You are order and rhythm and ritual. You are the alchemy that directs etheric forces. You are the Creator of the Sacred Temple.

May your energies merge with all the Divine Rays…creating swirling rainbow rings of universal tone and vibration.

All seven bowls are played now, one after the other…

Sitting in the presence of this powerful vortex of creational energies, we breathe deeply…absorbing these radiations…integrating their heightened frequencies into every cell of our body…so that our body becomes a Living Vessel for the Tones of Creation. As the healing powers of the Seven Rays bathe us, we receive any attunement or realignment that we may require at this time.

And now we visualize this beautiful living wheel of multi-coloured rays as a revolving disk of blazing colours that forms a forcefield which bathes all of life - elemental, animal, human - within its field. Slowly it begins to rise up and expand outward, riding on a carrier wave of sound to envelope the area we live in…as this spiraling ring of colour continues to grow, it encompasses the whole country…until finally the entire earth is encircled in this revolving rainbow sphere. We hold this vision setting the intention for Peace, Unity and Harmony to be reestablished throughout our universe of creation. We see the Seven Rays, alive with their pulsing, swirling tones, spiraling through the Galaxies, and all the manifest and unmanifest levels of the Cosmos, impulsing all consciousness with the urge to evolve.

Crystal sound fades into silence…

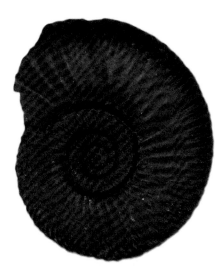

"Sound Is Like Sweetgrass
It Travels In Between Worlds"

From *Contact from the Underworld*
Robbie Robertson

Peruvian Whistling Vessels

ANCIENT SOUNDS RESURRECTED

As we surrender to our unfolding path, whatever we truly need has a way of finding us. So it was that I became introduced to the extraordinary psychoacoustic phenomenom of Peruvian Whistling Vessels. The clay vessels used today are replicas of ancient Andean artifacts which were a part of the Peruvian culture for a span of more than 2,000 years, from 500 B.C. until the time of the Spanish conquest of Peru in 1532, at which time they seemed to vanish. Perhaps "seemed to go underground" would be a more accurate description. They have recently reemerged thanks to Daniel Statnekov who rediscovered these sacred instruments of consciousness, resurrecting them for use in the 20th and 21st Centuries.

I first encountered their other-worldly tones at a sound healing intensive in Colorado. The experience was profound. When a group of seven vessels are played simultaneously in ceremony; the slight differential in their harmonic frequencies creates a sensation of sound inside the player's head unlike any other on earth. Soon after we began playing the vessels, I found myself transported at supersonic speed into an altered state of consciousness; sounds of wind whistling across the desert sands and buzzing insects filled my head. It evoked instantaneous recognition; an ancient Soul deja vu. I heard what sounded like many voices chattering inside my head all at once and just as I felt as though my head might burst, I surrendered and allowed the frequencies to carry me through a gateway. In this new space I discovered that I was able to distinguish distinct, individual voices...voices of wisdom which spoke to my Soul. I felt a profound comfort, like the joy of arriving home after a long absence. When the ceremony came to a close, we sat in silence and I could clearly hear the sounds of a rainstick softly cascading inside my ears. From this heightened state of hearing I was now acutely aware of the subtlest of sounds arising from within my own head.

The vessels' maker, Daniel Statnekov provides this explanation in *The Hummingbird Clue:*

"*By themselves, each whistle is not remarkable. The sound that they make approximates the sound made by the whistle of a tea kettle at full boil. What is noteworthy about the ancient whistles is the interaction of their sounds. Because they are very closely pitched, when they are played together they create low frequency difference tones or 'beat' frequencies in the brain. These are perceived as a low, fluttering hum, a sound that most closely resembles the sound of a hummingbird in flight. Acousticians categorize these sounds as 'phantom' tones that do not have a reality in the physical dimension. They are only created by our hearing apparatus and our brain. They are a creation of consciousness...*

"When a half-dozen or more of these whistles are played together the effect is aural 3-D that floods the mind with the sound of oceans and wind, the murmur of voices speaking in tongues, and a sensation that feels like no-voltage electricity surging from one side of the skull to the other. The totality of the effect gives participants a sense of the space inside of their head, and the tides of sound seem to sweep the mind clear of thought."

When I play the vessels, I feel currents of pulsating frequency moving in a figure eight formation as they loop between the left and right sides of my brain. The sensation is that of a spiraling funnel of sound in my head that seems to be performing a vacuuming function as it removes dense energies from my whole body. Through this process the vessels act as etheric purifiers, loosening, dislodging, and cleaning away the energies that we are ready to release.

"*In the Andean area the bird is a symbol for spiritual flight and in the earlier cultures the bird most frequently depicted is the macaw parrot. In Quechua (the Inca Language), the name for a macaw parrot is huacamaya. Whistling vessels are known as huacas, a generic term denoting something holy or sacred, and huacamaya means 'guardian of the sacred.'*"

From *Ancient Sound: The Whistling Vessels of Peru*
Daniel K. Statnekov

SACRED BREATH

When a group gathers to play the vessels, it is an intimate experience of co-creation. As Daniel expressed to me, *"the playing of these vessels together is a sacred thing…you are consciously co-mingling your breaths into a new creation."* While playing the vessels, a group's combined focus creates a unified field through which deep and transformational change can be initiated. The effects are far reaching, healing on personal, group, and planetary levels.

One of the greatest teachings I have received from the vessels is a deep appreciation for the sacredness of our breath. In Daniel's words, *"Your breath is precious…more precious than anything any of us can make or collect to put into the clay and fire, so when you put your breath into the vessel you should know that you are adding the most precious ingredient."* The secret the vessels impart is so simple it can evade us: we breathe in the love ~ we allow it to infuse our body ~ we breathe this love out through all the manifest and unmanifest planes. Our breath is a potent, enlivening power.

"Playing these instruments requires an attentive direction of your breath…
As you play, listen to the whistle. Hear it as a reflection of your inner energy flowing into the outer world."

From *Animated Earth*
Daniel K. Statnekov

Hidden within the inner passageway of each vessel a secret heart chamber has been handcarved, a reminder from their maker that every breath flowing through the vessel is imprinted with our heart's energy. Indeed, the vessels are holders of the vital life force, the prana, of our breath. Energetically they embody the vibration of the one who plays them.

LIVING SOUND CHAMBERS

As with the crystal bowls, a special magic is experienced when the whistling vessels are played in nature. One such occasion involved a vessel ceremony with friends who had gathered on a mountainside under the full moon, to celebrate the Fall Equinox. As we played, I experienced the merging of the sound of my breath blowing through the vessel with the powerful breath of the wind howling over the mountain. No longer able to distinguish the wind's breath from my own, wind and breath became one.

Given how accustomed I was to playing crystal bowls directly on the body as an energy attunement, it seemed only natural to apply this practice to the whistling vessels. During an evening gathering held high on a rocky outcrop under the stars, a group of six took turns playing the vessels on the various chakra centers of each member of the group. The first to volunteer, I felt as though I was in the center of a humming beehive, being played or buzzed by many bees. All awareness of individual consciousness seemed to dissolve as I felt myself being brought into alignment and merging with the higher group mind of the hive.

When played inside natural acoustical chambers such as mountain and sea caves, the vessels provide an incredible gateway for connecting with the inner earth and other realms. One memorable experience occurred inside the "living sound chamber" of a magnificent old growth tree that I discovered with friends on the shores of a remote lake in Northern B.C.. Highlighted by the water's tones of aquamarine, azure, and turquoise, the breathtaking energy of this wilderness lake was like a pure, translucent crystal. Along its banks stood a beautiful, tall fir tree with a long, bare trunk and vibrant evergreen branches at its crown. At the base of the tree a doorway had been cut providing an entrance into its hollowed out trunk. The height inside the chamber was about seven feet, providing ample standing room for two of us to play the vessels. While serenaded by the deep tones of a didgeridoo being played outside the tree's base, we felt as though our legs had become extensions of the tree itself, like roots anchoring us deep into the earth. At the same time, the harmonics from our vessels echoed off the interior walls of the trunk, resonating with the living consciousness of this beautiful tree. We were encompassed in a loving womb that had become a sound transformation chamber, a time tunnel that, while holding our physical bodies securely, allowed our consciousness to soar. As we sounded the vessels, a physical trembling sensation accompanied our shifting awareness. Perhaps in a similar way, the ancient ones used trees that had been naturally hollowed by lightening, to travel dimensionally.

INVOCATION TO THE SACRED VESSELS

Oh Sacred Whistling Vessels,

you are a gift of the One Heart…

Instruments through which the Breath of Love will sound

to open the mind-locks of consciousness and restore Humanity's remembrance of the path Home.

Birthed into form as the Will of Spirit, your Father,

impressed upon the Creative Intelligence of Matter, your Mother,

and was fused together by a magnetic field of Love,

your Light Consciousness.

You have been molded with loving care

in accordance with the design of your ancestors,

to embody the ancient wisdoms and future visions of Humankind.

You are a mosaic woven of many frequencies: of earth, moss and pine needle

from the mountaintop…of salt and sand from the sea…

of crushed crystal bowl…of clay, mica, sprig of cedar and

the pure heart of a tiny white flower from your maker's garden…

elements resurrected into a new form to intone songs

of Unity, Peace and Freedom.

You have been forged with the Fire of Creation with essences of pine and cherry

and the prayers of those who dreamed you to life.

Within your atoms the Cosmic Flame sings

to unite the Divine spark in all cells with the acoustical vibrations

of the Kingdom of Light and the Flaming Sounds of

Illumination, Purification, and Transformation.

Hidden within your inner passageways,
a secret heart chamber has been carved by your maker
to imprint every breath which flows through you with Love…
For it is this vital essence ~
the Breath of Life, the Breath of Sacred Intention ~
upon which your wings of sound will send Souls soaring
across the dimensions of time and space
and through the gateways of the Higher Worlds.

Oh Sacred Whistling Vessels of the One Heart,
you are charged with a great destiny to fulfill…
You are dedicated to lifting the veils of separation
and awakening the Higher Wisdom in all.
You will whistle across the land
and through the starry fields of space
sounding your Seven Sacred Tones and
emanating the Seven Rays of Creation…
your vibrational waves calling forth the telluric forces
from the four corners of the earth,
gathering Souls, whistling people awake,
activating the Crystal Cities of Light
and creating a Rainbow Bridge of Sound
upon which the Divine Plan will be unfolded,
the Future revealed, and the Higher Evolution realized.

May all who join in ceremony to receive your powerful medicine,
remember their eternal connection with All That Is,
and how with every precious breath they give,
they are empowering the Sacred Dream…
May all who hear the sounds of your calling
enter through the doorway of the Great Mystery
and be united in the Presence of
the One Will,
the One Heart,
the One Life.

"A sound is coming from the Eternal Abode to call you back."

Tulsi Sahib

"Seek the Sound that never ceases.

Seek the Sun that never sets."

Rumi

THE AUDIBLE LIFESTREAM

"The energies of the earth, the forces of the earth,
the sentient life in the earth, the consciousness life in the earth -
all are held together as one life within the great Sound Current."

From *Kundaline West*
Ann Ree Colton

*F*lowing in the earth beneath our feet, throughout every cell in our body, and permeating all realms is a stream which echoes everywhere and yet remains invisible and inaudible to most. As Hafiz Sahib exclaims, *"All the seven regions are resounding with this Sound. But fools do not hear It, for the Sound is subtle."* This current is always moving; it is alive with a radiance that sustains all life. It is a Divine River of Vibration emanating with the Consciousness that pervades all created form. This spiritual sound vibration is the primordial, magnetic lifeforce of creation; the sound of the Godhead in action. It is the keynote upon which the Universe is built.

How does one begin to define the undefinable? *"It is a language which has never been spoken or written. It is the ever-living melody that cannot be recorded on bars and spaces. Its notes are beyond the strings of any earthly instruments. Its inspiring chorus rings through every chamber of the soul, but there is no way to convey the idea to other people who have not heard it."* answers Julian Johnson in *The Path of the Masters.*

The Sound Current is known by many names: the Sanskrit word for it is "Shabd", it is also referred to as the Holy Spirit (Bible), the Audible Lifestream or the Divine Sound (Upanishads), the Naam or Holy Word (Sikh), the Music of the Spheres (Pythagoras), the Eternal Sound or Sound-Which-Comes-From-The-Skies (Muslim), the Voice of the Silence (Madame Blavatsky), the Celestial Sound (Mohammed), the Lost Word (Masonic Order), the Voice of God (Sufi)…

The Sound Current is much like a river that flows in all directions, both to and from the ocean. We are like the salmon returning on the stream, following the pure subtle sounds that guide our Soul to its ultimate destination. In *From Light to Sound*, Dennis Holtje explains, "*This Current's two main aspects actually resemble a great wave of motion and sound. Its first aspect is the out-flowing, circular wave that emerges from the Godhead to sustain life on all planes of experience. The second aspect is the returning wave, which returns through the created worlds and back to the bosom of God.*"

Julian Johnson expands this vision, "*This Current must not be understood to be like a river running in one course. It is more like a radio wave flowing out in every direction from the grand central broadcasting station. In fact, it comes from the supreme creative center of the Universe of Universes.*

"*This wave has two aspects, a centrifugal flow and a centripetal flow. It moves outward from the central dynamo of all creation, and it flows back toward that dynamo. Moving upon that Current, all power and all life appear to flow outward to the uttermost bounds of creation, and again upon it all life appears to be returning toward its source.*"

He continues with his description of the Audible Life Stream as a "*…divine current, wave or stream going forth from God himself and flowing throughout the Universe. It is not only an emanation from God but it is God himself.*

"*When any man speaks in this world, he simply sets in motion atmospheric vibrations. But when God speaks, He not only sets in motion etheric vibrations, but He himself moves in and through those vibrations. In truth it is God himself that vibrates all through infinite space. God is not static, latent: He is superlatively dynamic. When He speaks, everything in existence vibrates, and that is the Sound, the Shabd; and it can be heard by the inner ear, which has been trained to hear it. It is the divine energy in process of manifestation which is the Holy Shabd. It is, in fact, the only way in which the Supreme One can be seen and heard - this mighty, luminous and musical wave, creating and enchanting.*"

"The Nada is the grand symphony out of which all other symphonies flow. It is the primal music of the Universe. Every musical chord of this world is an echo of that primal chord."

From *The Path of the Masters*
Julian Johnson

"The whole Universe is resounding with the Sound, and thou hast only to open the door of thine ears.

"For opening the ears, it is sufficient to stop hearing the outer sounds. If you do this, you will hear the perpetual and unending Sound. It is Infinite and has no beginning nor end, and on account of that, It is called Anhad (i.e., without any limits). Without this Word - the Eternal Sound - an expression of the Infinite, the world could not have come into existence. Hold communion with the Melodious Sound and lose yourself in it, O wise man."

Shah Niaz

*"Within thee is Light and within the Light
the Sound,
and the same shall keep thee attached to the True One."*

Gurbani

"'Shabd' implies the Power of God that has created and is sustaining the various grand divisions, divisions and subdivisions of the vast creation of God. It is a current from the Ocean of Consciousness and is characterized by Sound-vibration, or in other words, It is a live and active principle which, emanating from God, is enlivening all creation. It is the instrument with which God creates, controls and sustains His vast Universe. It acts as a life-line between the Creator and His creation and serves as a golden bridge between the two. The divine currents, like the ethereal waves of a radio, are spread out in the atmosphere in all the directions of the compass, giving out delectable strains of music. We, however, cannot catch the ethereal vibrations and listen to the divine melody until we get in tune with the Infinite by adjusting our mental apparatus. Therefore we become etherealized more and more as we come in tune with the heavenly music. Shabd is the connecting link between God and man. In brief, Shabd alone is the true religion - a binding force that rebinds us to our Source. All the powers of Nature depend on and work through this Shabd or the Sound Principle. The Pranas or the vital airs, that are the source of all energy - electrical, mechanical, magnetic or atomic - and are the most active agents in the physical material plane, are but an outer manifested form of the Shabd. Like the electric waves with which the whole atmosphere is charged, Shabd in Its most subtle form pervades everywhere in Its fullness and is thus the Creator."

From *Naam or Word*
Kirpal Singh

"The music of the heavens is a delight to the inner ear… it is none other than the steadfast voice of God, echoing through the world of worlds, in a tumult of infinite variations, each embodying a unique aspect of God's beingness.

"It is the authentic verifiable presence of God, transformed into audible sound, which is the vibrating flow of atoms from the ocean of love and mercy, down to the lowest strata in the makeup of all its creation, the physical world, where it is disguised in the vibrant piping of a bird, the giggling trill of little children, or the muffled sound of your own heartbeat.

"All that is living has life by the grace of this music, but only the inner travellers, the initiates, have been allowed glimpses behind the veil of form, into the secret mysteries of light and sound and vibration which lie at the core of all we perceive.

"It is the transformation of God's voice into audible form which accounts for man's ability to reach the heights and scale the precipice of divine illumination.

"The sound of the spiritual current is not only uplifting in its tone and melodic content, but carries within it the miraculous qualities of the source Itself, which is more uplifting than anything man can reconstruct with his physical instrument. The sound current carries with it wisdom, power and love in the freshest state, and Soul drinks of it like an infant at its mother's breast, gaining and strengthening in these qualities which are its very own."

From *From the Temple Within*
Evan T. Pritchard

THE HEALING CURRENT

The Eternal Sound Current is the primal creative essence behind everything. It is the fountainhead of God's Love which can remove our sufferings at the root. As primary manifestations of the Original Vibration, Sound and Light are inherent in one another. Indian Sikh Guru Nanak described, *"In the heart of the Light within is a delectable Sound, that makes one fully absorbed in God"*.

In this excerpt from *From Light to Sound*, Dennis Holtje offers a passionate commentary on sound's intrinsic role: *"...much more than listening to beautiful sounds or music, spiritual attunement to the Sound Current within is the process for liberating soul from the clutches of mind, emotion, and illusion. This way of spiritual attainment and enlightenment far outstrips what can be gained spiritually through following the spiritual energy of the light. While information and knowledge - the fruits of pursuing the light - provide relative levels of peace and spiritual progress, they pale in comparison to the higher God attributes of true love, wisdom, freedom, and power which the awakened Sound Current imbues within the sincere seeker of truth. These divine attributes which are enlivened through bathing in the Audible Life Stream, transform the seeker of truth into a doer of truth.*

"The Sound can heal the deep-seated karmic conditions that limit all seekers and keep us from experiencing the contact with the God within, which we so fervently desire. Where the light can reveal truth to the seeker's eyes, the Sound actualizes what the light reveals...The explanation of this lies in the light itself. Originating in the mental body and stationed and active within the energy centers of our physical bodies, the light element of the Audible Life Stream deals with thought, feeling, and personal will... Healings which come through a change of mind or feeling instigated by personal will, simply do not have the sustaining power to be permanent or complete. True healings require the action and true transformational ability of Sound...

"Sound is the spiritual energy that enlivens soul, not the mind. Awakening the Sound Current awakens the essence of soul, and all life changes for the seeker."

Dennis continues: *"When the light has served its purpose in our spiritual development, the Sound appears...The purpose of the light is to reveal our own entrapment; the transcendency of Sound lies in its power to free the ensnared soul."* Hence realization is attained through the drinking of the combined elixirs of Divine Sound and Light: the Light which is the Revealer and the Sound which is the Liberator, the Deliverer of freedom.

"The Audible Sound Current can be felt as an outgoing, expanding, pulsing, ecstatic joy emanating from the eyebrow center. When the triune powers of seeing, hearing and speaking are activated, the physical senses are muted and made quiescent. The lower aspects of the senses become as lowered flames in a lamp, while the innermost light of the mind sees, hears, and speaks of the Real.

True inner hearing has not been perfected until one can hear the sound in a seed, in a leaf, in a tree, in a grain of sand, in a flower, in its fruit, in a mountain, in a rainbow, in a drop of rain. When one unites with the Archetone giving life to all forms of life, he unites with the Cosmic Music of the Universe. Finally, one unites with the tone of his own direct star from whence he came."

From *The Archetypal Kingdom*
Ann Ree Colton

144

"And I heard a voice from heaven
like the sound of many waters and
like the sound of loud thunder;
the voice I heard was like the sound
of harpers playing on their harps."

Revelation 14:2

HEARING THE SOUND CURRENT

*H*ow do we make contact with the Sound Current? *"The Sublime Sound cannot of course be heard by the physical ears. There is a way for our listening to the divine Music which can be heard by the inner faculty of transcendental hearing"* advises Kirpal Singh in *Naam or Word.*

When our consciousness is focused on the material world we cannot hear the Great Sound. One must cease listening to all external sounds by deeply centering the self within one's inner chamber: the cave of mystic hearing associated with the pineal gland. Centuries ago, French philosopher Rene Descartes identified the pineal gland as the location in the body where "mankind and God meet". Accessing our ability to hear transcendentally requires the unwavering gathering of all one's energy upon this point, closing all outer doors, and opening the inner ears. Here, the combined focus of one's etheric ears and Third Eye upon the vast stillness of Silence will eventually pierce the walls of the mind and open the vibrational channel for contact.

Julian Johnson offers the following instructions on this Yogic discipline, *"…the Masters speak of closing the nine doors of the outer world. The nine doors referred to are: the two eyes, the two ears, the two nostrils, the mouth, the sex organ, the rectum.*

"These are the chief means of holding communication with the outer world. All these must be closed - that is, all attention must be removed from them…

"When every ray of attention is inside, concentrated at the proper center, with no wavering thought lingering outside, then the student is in a position to get results. He must get results. He cannot fail to get them. He will at first experience flashes of light or hear sounds - perhaps both. But no matter what he sees or hears, he should not allow his mind to wonder from the center. In other words, he must never go out after any sound or sight. Let them come to him at the center. If you leave the center, you will lose the lights and sounds also. By and by, with the gathering of all the life currents of the body at the center, the powers of the mind and soul will greatly increase."

Describing the absolute beauty of the sounds awaiting us, Julian continues, *"Try now to get a picture of that Luminous Reality, the Grand Orchestra of the Universe. Its heavenly strains are not only filling all interstellar space but they are ringing with far more enchanting music through all the higher worlds beyond the utmost bounds of the physical. The higher we go, the more enchanting the music. In those higher worlds the music is less mixed with matter, and so it is not dulled…There is not a cubic millimeter of space in existence which is not filled with this music. Sweeter and sweeter its heavenly strains vibrate through every living being, great or small, from world to world, and from Universe to Universe. Its life-giving melodies may not be consciously heard by those who are not trained to catch them, but there is not a living being in all creation which does not derive its life from this Current. All joy that has ever thrilled a living soul has come out of this Divine Harmonic. How great is this Luminous Reality!"*

As the soul ascends upon its journey along the Sound Current, a series of elemental sounds, each designating a specific spiritual region, become audible to the inner ear. These have been documented by spiritual masters from different traditions with remarkable similarity. They include descriptions of an ascending ladder of sounds: the pounding surf of the sea, the humming of bees, the tinkling of soft bells, the running water of a brook, the chirping of crickets, the rumbling of thunder, the roaring of a lion, the ringing of a loud bell, the blowing of a conch shell, the gong of a big drum, the strings of a harp, the tone of a flute, the sound of bagpipes, the absence of all sound, and then the Great Soundless Sound which permeates all others.

The keys to all kingdoms exist within us. When our lower bodies (physical, emotional and mental) are brought into alignment with our Soul, and we access the inner faculty of our transcendental hearing, the Great Universal Sound may reveal itself, bathing us in its infinite ocean.

"...*a creative responsiveness to
the music of the spheres will bring forth
the new music*"

From *The Rays and the Initiations*
Alice A. Bailey

THE WAY OF
CONSCIOUS EVOLUTION

SOUND CODINGS OF THE DIMENSIONS

Listening to the birds call in spring, I hear the many levels from which they operate. Not only are they singing to call forth new buds on the trees and coax forward new shoots from the ground, they are in fact delivering a message to all life on earth, "Awaken, awaken, it is time to create new life!" All of the natural world hears and obeys this wake up call. Will we have the ears to hear the messages of Higher Evolution being impulsed to us through beautiful birdsong? Will we respond to the call of the Divine Plan that ceaselessly sings out to us? In *The Pleiadian Agenda,* Barbara Hand Clow discusses how specific higher dimensions may be accessed through the sound codes of nature:

> *"...tuning into 7D could be facilitated by studying bird intonations because 7D is the dimension that causes human language to be so sound coded. Birdsong is actually higher dimensional than the sound coding of human language! All the uneven dimensions - 1D through 9D - are sound coded. The structure of sound actually holds them in form, and these vibrations generate creativity! For example, the 1D sound of Earth is a low hum that manifests as swamp song and low frequency sound in the ground, and this is what keeps your hearts beating while you are alive. John Michell has demonstrated that the harmony of cultures is maintained or destroyed by chanting. Higher dimensions can be directly apprehended in 3D by means of selected music, such as Bach cello sonatas or string quartets by Beethoven. Toning in 3D accesses 5D resonance, and 7D music of the spheres can be heard by lying on the ground and vibrating with the Earth bathed in starlight when there is absolute silence.... Seventh-dimensional sound is birdsong, wind, photons moving in great 7D bands, and the solar wind. Ninth dimensional sound emerges out of the absolute silence and darkness of the Galactic Center, which is moving in a slow, circular motion."*

HIGHER CONSCIOUSNESS SOUND

"…no one will halt the Rebirth of Pure Music:
one cannot stop the cosmic river of human history."

From *The Secret Music of the Soul*
Patrick Berndardt

"….the study of sound and the effect of sound will put into man's hands a tremendous instrument in the world of creation.
Through the use of sound the scientist of the future will bring about his results; through sound, a new field of discovery will open up; the
sound which every form in all kingdoms of nature gives forth will be studied and known and changes will be brought about and new
forms developed through its medium. One hint only may I give here and that is, that the release of energy in the atom is linked to this
new coming science of sound."

From *A Treatise on White Magic*
Alice A. Bailey

"Through the evolutionary process all manifestations are tuning with each other in such harmony that eventually there will be a Cosmic symphony in which every individual, nation, globe and solar system is in harmony with the whole symphony."

From *Symphony of the Zodiac*
Torkom Saraydarian

"When all the cells of the cosmos, all planets, all civilizations throughout the galaxy will vibrate in harmony, free from egotistic or anarchic desires, following the directives of the Great Universal Conductor by seeking the beauty of the whole - and not merely for the pleasure of one minute part to the detriment of others - the immense cosmic symphony will be heard in all planes of existence and the living beings of all kingdoms will once again find the eternal rhythm of love, the celestial melody of the music of the soul. Such is the infinite goal of evolution."

From *The Secret Music of the Soul*
Patrick Bernhardt

"A time will come when the children will gather and, using their unique telepathy, make silent sound. They will use their minds to create symphonies on other dimensions of existence. They will use sound internally and externally to create harmonics as light shields all over the planet...

"Many will awaken to the use of sound. There will be major discoveries and energy impacts using sound. If one hundred thousand individuals are impulsed to harmonize, and allow themselves to be played harmoniously as instruments of consciousness - imagine! Everything comes from sound. Sound is the primal energy that is used to create. Sound came first."

From *Earth Pleiadian Keys to the Living Library*
Barbara Marciniak

"To create the Age of Aquarius, music must go beyond the level of naive entertainment to reach the sphere of the spirit. It will be the breath of consciousness; it will become the song of souls by echoing their highest intuitions, it being so true that through it, the soul's life manifests itself in this world. New composers will once again hear the grandiose symphony vibrating in the galaxy and their creations will awaken the superior responsibility of the human form...

The new composers will not only be virtuosos; they will be genuine mystics. Their mission will surpass the role of public entertainers and they will recover the great initiatory work of the creators of sacred music. Insofar as their music will put human beings into contact with the devic, edenic and spiritual spheres, they will allow men to once again hear the great cosmic breath and to physically feel the supra-natural presence that each of us bears within us through eternity."

From *The Secret Music of the Soul*
Patrick Bernhardt

In *The Creative Fire*, author, musician and beloved teacher of the Ageless Wisdom, Torkom Saraydarian shares his vision of music for the future:

"*New Era musicians are beginning to incarnate. Some of them will compose music for the mysteries of initiations; some of them will work on other dimensions. Some of them will work to compose special music for the healing of every disease in each part of the human body.*

"*More advanced musicians will work to align the Planetary Life with the Solar and Galactic Life.*

"*Music in the coming centuries will play a greater role than the roles played by physics, chemistry, and engineering combined. Through the utilization of sound, many scientific discoveries will be rendered obsolete. It will be possible through music to lead nations and humanity to a higher realization of divine principles.*"

He describes the various dimensional levels from which music can be created:

"1. *On the first dimension, music is composed to give us emotional pleasure. Rhythmic music creates pleasure in our emotional nature, and many musicians are just interested in creating that pleasure.*

2. *On the second dimension, music is composed for some idea, or to make a breakthrough into a higher level, mostly using rhythm and melody.*

3. *On the third dimension, music is composed to bring healing to the physical, emotional, and mental natures.*

4. *On the fourth dimension, music is composed to manifest the rhythm of the energies behind the manifested Universe and to create alignment with them.*

5. *On the fifth dimension, it is composed to initiate the soul into his higher destiny.*

6. *On the sixth dimension, music is used to protect the Pilgrim on the higher path from dark attacks.*

7. *On the seventh dimension, music is composed to reveal the Divine Mysteries.*

8. *On the eighth dimension, music is used to express gratitude to the highest Glory.*"

"The Magi of sound and music will be Those Who will have electronics, chemistry, musical, and inspirational backgrounds. They will be scientists. They will be able to receive inspiration from higher sources of music, and also They will have enough preparation to receive impressions of supreme ideas which will be put into musical forms.

"Music will be used to create harmony and cooperation and peace in the world. The purpose of music in the future is to do the following:

1. Invigorate the cells and atoms in the vehicles of man
2. Create integration and health
3. Stimulate the glands and chakras through expanding the consciousness
4. Eradicate disorders and attacks to the body, emotions, and mental nature
5. Protect the vehicles of man from attacks of germs and hostile viruses in Nature
6. Provide 'sunshine and food' for the chakras to bloom in harmonious ways
7. Stimulate sensitivity in the emotions and clarity and sharpness in the mind
8. Increase striving and labor for perfection
9. Encourage heroic acts, fearlessness, and daring
10. Create a breakthrough between the visible and the Subtle Worlds
11. Enable man to have contact with his heart and conscience and to reveal the sense of responsibility
12. Cause the blooming of his Chalice
13. Realize the brotherhood of humanity
14. Realize one's own divinity
15. Develop forgiveness, gratitude, and bliss

"To actualize such a vision, a new breed of composers will soon appear in the world, and the science of sound, with all its mysteries, will be available to them."

From *The Creative Sound*
Torkom Saraydarian

"The Ageless Wisdom says that before conception takes place the human soul releases his creative note upon which his vehicles form themselves. And when the time of departure comes, the human soul stops sounding the note and the disintegration of the bodies takes place.

"The Ageless Wisdom says that 'the One began to sound His note and the manifestation of the Universe began.' Soon we will find that all manifestation is a condensed sound. It is on the keynote of creation that all forms of life are striving in order to reach perfection — a supreme state of health.

"The keynote, the nature of our essential pitch, the pure sound of our being is ever expanding, liberating, and inclusive. To discover this note and to create harmonious cords within all our systems is the process of advanced healing of the future."

From *New Dimensions in Healing*
Torkom Saraydarian

"Some day music will be the means of expressing universal religion.
There will come a day when music and its philosophy will become the religion of humanity."

From *Music of Life*
Hazrat Inayat Khan

FUTURE VISIONS

The etheric winds of change are blowing with determination across the earth. They are propelled by the ever-driving force of Evolution that urges humanity along its path. What are we evolving toward? Beneath the visible chaos manifesting in our world, a highly organized Plan of Infinite Wisdom *is* unfolding.

The unprecedented awakening of consciousness taking place on earth signals our initiation into a new level of Evolution. We are participating in a momentous act of creation: the birth of a new awareness, our Cosmic Consciousness.

The inclusion of sound meditation into our daily practice can assist us in this process by expanding our inner awareness, raising our vibratory field, and allowing for the:

~ Conscious, intentional visioning of new potentials for ourselves and our world.
~ Clearing of sensory overload (from television and computers) that clutters our consciousness and suppresses our natural creativity.
~ Purification of our energy fields.
~ Cultivation of the gardens of creative awareness within our minds so that our dreams and life's purpose can take seed, flourish and be actualized.
~ Alignment of our will with the Divine and an increasing willingness and ability to serve.

As our vibratory rate increases, we become more receptive to the stimulation and purification of the Higher Energies. Sound creates a bridge that reaches the Highest Realms. The joyful, transformative power of sound, made with intention, offers a natural way of shifting our frequency to the ever-expanding energies of Creation which are an inherent part of us. This higher creational work requires a balance of both silence and sound, for it is within the Silence that the Great Sound is heard.

We live in a Harmonic Universe. Not only is our world comprised of sound, even the vacuum of space is full of sound which exists as electromagnetic vibrations: the solar winds interacting with the planets, the droning of pulsating stars. Every dimension of existence is an interplay of the frequencies of sound, light and geometry. Frequency or vibration are the keys which open the gates of higher consciousness.

We are, at our very Core, sound, which is magnetic. It is the binding force of love that links together the atoms of the form world. Through the streaming chords of vibration, sound and colour, the Cosmic Creation continues to unfold and evolve. Working with our Inner Essence, in accordance with the One Will, we can become true creators with sound. When we create from the purity of our Souls, for the good of the whole rather than simply the fulfillment of personal ego desire, we will receive our full remembrance of how to utilize the power of sound to heal our physical bodies and bring into manifestation all that is needed to fulfill our service. We will create a world of beauty and unity…out of Harmony.

A Future Vision:

In the future we will apply harmonic architecture utilizing dome and pyramid formations to build magnificent Sound Temples. These vibrational healing chambers will unite sound harmonics, colour and sacred geometry. They will be designed on power spots in nature where the earth grids align, enhancing both their receiving and transmitting qualities. Within these sacred spaces ceremonial attunements to the Cosmos will take place….gatherings for receiving the inflow of cosmic energies during the key impulses of new and full moons, celebrations of spring and fall equinoxes, summer and winter solstices, solar and lunar eclipses, as well as daily ceremonies of life acknowledging the creative cycle within each sunrise and sunset.

These Sound Temples will function as magnetic beacons and focal points for concentrating cosmic and solar energies within their form as well as broadcasting energies of healing, beauty, regeneration and peace around the planet. They will be spaces where the New Cosmic Music will be birthed…music which is a fusion of voice and pure sound…of overtones and mantras and chants…of crystal singing bowls, whistling vessels, harps, flutes, drums and gongs …of birdsong, windsong, cricketsong, the songs of brooks and oceans…the sighing of Mother Earth as She rests at night…and of Celestial Starsong…as we lay our bodies upon the earth and, gazing upward into the starry realms, listen to the worlds of tones resounding through the Constellations of the Cosmos…serenading us into the Temples of Higher Learning that we visit during our dreamtime.

Those who hear and respond to the Great Call are pioneers of the Higher Evolution. Our work with Higher Consciousness Sound represents the striving, the aspiration, and the destiny of our Souls. We will bring in the new future with the Voice of our Soul, sung in harmony with nature and the laws of the universe.

"The PEACE for which every soul strives, and which is the true nature of God
and the utmost goal of man, is but the outcome of Harmony."

From *The Mysticism of Sound*
Hazrat Inayat Khan

"The secret consists in practice
And not in thinking and discussing.
Give up wrangling and do the practice.
Then you will know the secret."

Kabir

"No more words.
Hear only the Voice within."

Rumi

Agni Yoga Society. *Fiery World I,* New York, NY: Agni Yoga Society, Inc., 1933.

Aivanhov, Omraam Mikhael. *Angels and other Mysteries of The Tree of Life,* Frejus Cedex, France: Editions Prosveta, 1995.

Baer, Randall N. & Vicki V. *The Crystal Connection,* San Francisco, CA: Harper & Row, 1987.

Bailey, Alice A. *A Treatise on Cosmic Fire,* New York, N.Y.: Lucis Publishing Company, 1925.

Bailey, Alice A. *A Treatise on White Magic,* New York, N.Y.: Lucis Publishing Company, 1934.

Bailey, Alice A. *Initiation Human and Solar,* New York, N.Y.: Lucis Publishing Company, 1922.

Bailey, Alice A. *Letters on Occult Meditation,* New York, N.Y.: Lucis Publishing Company, 1922.

Bailey, Alice A. *The Rays and The Initiations,* New York, N.Y.: Lucis Publishing Company, 1960.

Bernhardt, Patrick. *The Secret Music of the Soul,* Ste. Adele, Quebec: Imagine Records & Publishing, 1991.

Blavatsky, H. P. *The Voice of the Silence,* Pasedena, CA: Theosophical University Press, 1889.

Clow, Barbara Hand. *The Pleiadian Agenda,* Santa Fe, NM: Bear & Company Publishing, 1995.

Colton, Ann Ree. *Islands of Light,* Glendale, CA: Arc Publishing Co., 1981.

Colton, Ann Ree. *Kundalini West,* Glendale, CA: Arc Publishing Co., 1978.

Colton, Ann Ree. *The Archetypal Kingdom,* Glendale, CA: Arc Publishing Co., 1988.

Dewhurst-Maddock, Olivea. *The Book of Sound Therapy,* New York, NY: Simon & Shuster Inc., 1993.

Godwin, Joscelyn. *The Mystery of the Seven Vowels,* Grand Rapids, MI: Phanes Press, 1991.

Govinda, Lama. *Creative Meditation and Multi-Dimensional Consciousness,* Wheaton, IL: Quest Books, 1976.

Govinda, Lama. *Foundations of Tibetan Mysticism,* London, England: Rider, 1969.

Gray, William. *The Ladder of Lights,* York Beach, ME: Samuel Weiser, 1981.

Heindel, Max. *The Rosicrucian Cosmo-Conception,* Oceanside, CA: The Rosicrucian Fellowship, 1998.

Hodson, Geoffrey, *The Kingdom of the Gods,* Adyar, India: Theosophical Publishing House, 1952.

Holtje, Dennis, *From Light to Sound: The Spiritual Progression,* Albuquerque, NM: MasterPath Inc., 1995.

Hurtak, J. J. *The Book of Knowledge: The Keys of Enoch,* Los Gatos, CA: The Academy For Future Science, 1977.

Johnson, Julian. *The Path Of The Masters,* Punjab, India: Radha Soami Satsang Beas, 1997.

Kenyon, Tom and Essene, Virginia. *The Hathor Material,* Santa Clara, CA: Spiritual Education Endeavours Publishing Company, 1996.

Keyes, Laurel Elizabeth. *Toning - The Creative Power of the Voice,* Marina del Rey, CA: DeVorss Publications, 1973.

Khan, Hazrat Inayat. *The Music of Life,* New Lebanon, NY: Omega Publications, 1983.

Khan, Hazrat Inayat. *The Mysticism of Sound and Music,* Boston, MA: Shambhala Publications, Inc., 1991.

Khan, Vilayat Inayat. *Toward the One,* New York, NY: Harper and Row Publishers, 1959.

Lewis, Robert C. *The Sacred Word and Its Creative Overtones,* Oceanside, CA: The Rosicrucian Fellowship, 1986.

Lu, Grandmaster Sheng-Yen. *The Inner World of the Lake,* San Bruno, CA: Amitabha Enterprises, Inc., 1992.

Maman, Fabian. *The Role of Music in the Twenty-First Century,* Redondo Beach, CA: Tama-Do Press, 1997.

Marciniak, Barbara. *Bringers of the Dawn,* Sante Fe, NM: Bear & Company Publishing, 1992.

Marciniak, Barbara. *Earth: Pleiadian Keys to the Living Library,* Bear & Company Publishing, 1995.

Marooney, Kimberly. *Angel Blessings,* Carmel, CA: Merrill-West Publishing, 1995.

Melville, Leinani. *Children of the Rainbow,* Wheaton, IL: Quest Books, 1969.

Muktananda, Swami. *I Am That,* South Fallsburg, NY: SYDA Foundation, 1992.

Odier, Daniel. *Tantric Quest: An Encounter with Absolute Love,* Rochester, VT: Inner Traditions International, 1997.

Pritchard, Evan. *From the Temple Within: The Fourth Book of Light,* Woodstock, NY: Resonance Communications, 1993.

Rael, Joseph & Marlow, Mary Elizabeth. *Being and Vibration,* San Francisco, CA: Council Oak Books, 1993.

Saraydarian, Torkom. *Aura – Shield of Protection & Glory,* Cave Creek, AZ: T.S.G. Publishing Foundation, Inc., 1999.

Saraydarian, Torkom. *Cosmos in Man,* Sedona, AZ: Aquarian Educational Group, 1973.

Saraydarian, Torkom. *The Creative Fire,* Cave Creek, AZ: T.S.G. Publishing Foundation, Inc., 1996.

Saraydarian, Torkom. *The Creative Sound,* Cave Creek, AZ: T.S.G. Publishing Foundation, Inc., 1999.

Saraydarian, Torkom. *New Dimensions in Healing,* Cave Creek, AZ: T.S.G. Publishing Foundation, Inc., 1992.

Saraydarian, Torkom. *Symphony of the Zodiac,* Cave Creek, AZ: T.S.G. Publishing Foundation, Inc., 1988.

Saraydatian, Torkom. *The Science of Meditation,* Cave Creek, AZ: The Creative Trust, 1993.

Singh, Kirpar. *Naam or Word,* Anaheim, CA: Ruhani Satsang, 1981.

St. Germain. *Earth's Birth Changes,* Scottsdale, AZ: Triad Prublishers USA, Inc., 1994.

Statnekov, Daniel K. *Animated Earth,* Berkeley, CA: North Atlantic Books, 1987.

Steiner, Rudoloph. *The Inner Nature of Music and the Experience of Tone,* Hudson, NY: Anthroposophic Press, 1983.

Yogananda, Paramahansa. *Autobiography of a Yogi,* Los Angeles, CA: Self-Realization Fellowship, 1998.

Yogananda, Paramahansa, *Journey to Self-realization,* Los Angeles, CA: Self-Realization Fellowship, 1997.

Yogananda, Paramahansa, *Metaphysical Meditations,* Los Angeles, CA: Self-Realization Fellowship, 1964.

Ywahoo, Dhyani. *Voices Of Our Ancestors,* Boston, MA: Shambhala Publications, Inc., 1987.

ACKNOWLEDGEMENTS

Grateful acknowledgement is made to the publishers and individuals listed below, for being granted permission to reprint images and excerpts from the following works:

IMAGES

Cover - *Nautilus Shell* © Deborah Van Dyke, 2001.

Page 15 - Photograph © Arnie Rosner 2000. Reprinted by permission of Arnie Rosner Enterprises, 8905 Rhine River Avenue, Fountain Valley, CA 92708-5607. http://arnierosner.com

Page 22 - Image from P.101, Cymatics, Vol.II, by Hans Jenny. Reprinted by permission of MACROmedia, P.O. Box 279, Epping, NH 03042. www.cymaticsource.com

Page 35 - *Inner Listening*, oil on canvas © Josh Van Dyke, 1999.

Page 39 - *Spirit Speaks*, oil on canvas © Josh Van Dyke, 1997.

Page 42 - *Water Ripple* © 2001. www.arttoday.com.

Page 58 - Image of *The World Mother*, Plate 29, from *The Kingdom of the Gods*, by Geoffrey Hodson. Reprinted by permission of The Theosophical Publishing House, Adyar, Chennai 600 020, India.

Page 95 - *Harmonic Union*, pencil and wash © Harold Pym, 1988. Salmon Arm, B.C., Canada.

Page 97 - Photograph © James Bell 1999. Reprinted by permission of James Bell.

Page 137 - *Waterfall*, oil on canvas © Josh Van Dyke, 1999.

Page 149 - *Totem*, oil on canvas © Josh Van Dyke, 1997.

Page 152 - *Planets*, oil on canvas © Josh Van Dyke, 1999.

Page 157 - *Pyramid*, watercolour © Josh Van Dyke, 1996.

All other photographs © Deborah Van Dyke, 2000.

EXCERPTS

Excerpts from Aura – Shield of Protection & Glory, Cosmos in Man, The Creative Fire, The Creative Sound, New Dimensions in Healing, The Science of Meditation, Symphony of the Zodiac, by Torkom Saraydarian. Reprinted by permission of T.S.G. Publishing Foundation, Inc. P.O. Box 7068, Cave Creek, AZ 85327. www.tsg-publishing.com

Excerpts from A Treatise on Cosmic Fire, A Treatise on White Magic, Initiation Human and Solar, Letters on Occult Meditation, The Rays and The Initiations, by Alice A. Bailey. These extracts are published with permission of Lucis Trust, which holds copyright, Lucis Publishing Company, New York, NY.

Excerpts from Being and Vibration, by Joseph Rael, with Mary Elizabeth Marlow used by permission of Council Oak Books, 1290 Chestnut Street, San Francisco, CA 94109. Copyright © 1993 by Joseph Rael and Mary Elizabeth Marlow.

Excerpts from The Temple Within: The Fourth Book of Light, by Evan Pritchard. Reprinted by permission of the author. Resonance Books, P.O. Box 1028, Woodstock, NY 12498.

Excerpts from Tantric Quest: An Encounter with Absolute Love, by Daniel Odier. Copyright © 1996, 1997 by Daniel Odier. Reprinted by permission of the publisher, Inner Traditions International, One Park Street, Rochester, VT 05767.

Excerpts from The Inner World of the Lake, by
Grandmaster Sheng-Yen Lu. Reprinted by permission
of Amitabha Enterprises, Inc., San Bruno, CA.

Excerpts from The Hathor Material, by Tom Kenyon and
Virginia Essene. Reprinted by permission of Spiritual
Education Endeavours Publishing Company, Santa
Clara, CA.

Excerpts from The Mystery of the Seven Vowels, by
Joscelyn Godwin. Reprinted by permission of Phanes
Press, Grand Rapids, MI.

Excerpts from Fiery World, Vol. I, by Agni Yoga Society.
Reprinted by permission of Agni Yoga Society, New
York, NY.

Excerpts from The Music of Life, by Hazrat Inayat Khan.
Reprinted by permission of Omega Publications, 256
Darrow Road, New Lebanon, NY 12125-2615,
www.omegapub.com

Excerpts from P. 27 and 94, The Mysticism of Sound and
Music, by Hazrat Inayat Khan. Reprinted by permis-
sion of Sufi Movement International Headquarters,
The Netherlands.